The Complete Book
of Color Healing

The Complete Book of Color Healing

PRACTICAL WAYS TO ENHANCE YOUR PHYSICAL AND SPIRITUAL WELL-BEING

Lilian Verner-Bonds

Edited by Dr. Ronald L. Bonewitz

A GODSFIELD BOOK

Library of Congress Cataloging-in-Publication
Data Available

10 9 8 7 6 5 4 3 2 1

Published in 2000 by
Sterling Publishing Company, Inc.
387 Park Avenue South, New York, N.Y. 10016

Distributed in Canada by Sterling Publishing
c/o Canadian Manda Group, One Atlantic Avenue,
Suite 105, Toronto, Ontario, Canada M6K 3E7
Distributed in Australia by Capricorn Link (Australia) Pty Ltd,
P O. Box 6651, Baulkham Hills, Business Centre,
NSW 2153, Australia

Designed for Godsfield Press by
THE BRIDGEWATER BOOK COMPANY

Photographer Mike Hemsley, Walter Gardiner Photography
Illustrations Kim Glass, Ian Mitchell, Andrew Kulman
Three-Dimensional Models Mark Jamieson

Printed and bound in China

ISBN 0–8069–8727-8

Picture Acknowledgments
The publishers would like to thank the following for the use of pictures:

Abode UK: 39, 91. *Corbis*: /Lester V Bergman 114BL;
/Bettmann 22, 42TR, 47; /Rodney Hyett 57; /Dave Kaup 26–27T;
Laslo Veres 71TR; /Adam Woolfitt 45T. *Liz Eddison*: 30, 62T, 63; *The Garden Picture
Library*: /John Glover 61. *The Image Bank*: /Patrick Curtet 7; /David De Lossy 81;
/Antony Edwards 51; /Eric Meola 17. *Science Photo Library*: /Garion Hutchings 18, 53T.
The Stock Market: /Jose L. Peleaz 28B; /Clayon J. Price 9. *Tony Stone*: /John Beatty 41;
/David Croland 24; /James Darell 23; /Peter Dokus 49; /Paul Grebiunas 33; /Donna
Kay 120; /Renee Lynn 90; /Laurence Monneret 82; /Peter Nicholson 21; /Victoria
Pearson 103; /Paul Redman 37; / Rick Rusing 107; /Andy Sacks 83; /Rosemary
Weller 100T and 135; /Charlie Westman 69; / Art Wolfe 118. *Trip*: 32;
/Dinodia 128BL; /Helene Rogers 19; /Tjagny-Rjadno 50L;
/Bob Turner 55; /N. and J. Wiseman 101.

Front Cover: The Stock Market/Pete Saloutos.

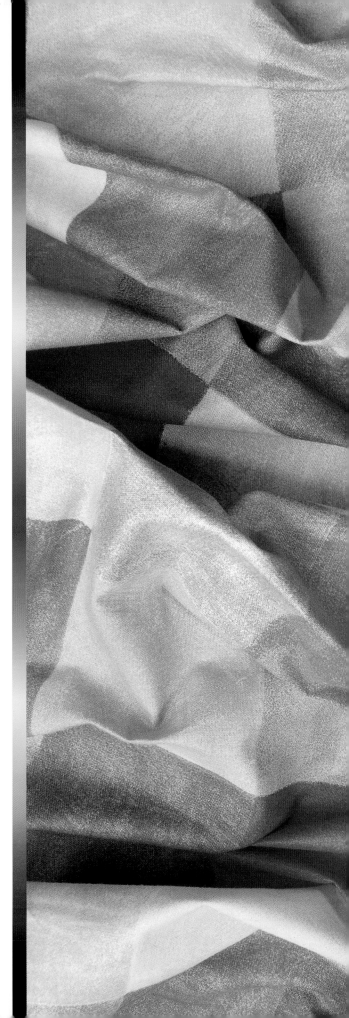

CONTENTS

INTRODUCTION

Color and life are inseparable. From the moment that we are born, and even before, color becomes part of the very substance of our lives. It is simply not possible to be indifferent to color. It has a practical bearing on our personal relationships, it affects the home environment and that of factories, offices, and hospitals. Even the color of your clothes is a personal calling card, affecting not only us but the people with whom we come into contact.

COLOR INFLUENCES everything we eat, drink, touch, and are surrounded by. It affects our moods and our emotions, it colors our personalities. We speak of having the blues, of golden opportunities, of seeing red; yet most of us take color for granted.

Ancient cultures, even into prehistory, have connected with and, in some cases, worshiped color. The bones of people buried tens of thousands of years ago have been found coated with red ocher, with colored stones and other objects buried with them. Many ancient peoples worshiped the sun, the source of all color, and harnessed its healing powers.

The origins of healing with color in the western world can be traced most directly back to ancient Egypt, where treatments were carried out in sanctuaries and temples. But in Egyptian practice, a medication was used because it was the same color as that produced by the ailment it was treating—purple medication for bruises, red medication for bleeding, and so on.

Modern color therapy is scientific, methodical, and rooted in long centuries of development, as we will discover in the following pages. Its effects have been explored by doctors, psychologists, psychiatrists, and neurologists, as well as color therapists.

The Benefits of Color

When we start to explore the world of color we realize there is more to it than meets the eye. Color can reveal the significance of actions that cannot otherwise be observed. Color goes beyond the surface. We can see with our eyes but color can see deeper and further.

Color comes from the light, and without light there is no life. From the brilliance of pure light come all the colors, each with their own individual impact upon our

systems mentally, emotionally, and physically. Color is all around us and affects our everyday life in countless ways. By enhancing our awareness of the power of color and the effect it has on our moods, emotions, and even performance, we can learn to use color to make positive changes in our lives. Many of our healing needs can be met by the use of color, which brings about harmony and balance within the psyche and body, while the invisible vibrations of color can either relax or stimulate us according to the colors chosen for healing.

Exploring color is a non-invasive way of discovering yourself. Color goes beyond itself. It has its own intelligence. Get to know what color can do for you—it can change your life.

Color yourself healthy, wealthy, and wise.

About This Book

In this book, we explore the history and development of color therapy, color connections to psychology, personality, and the physical body, and color's use in both physical and emotional healing. We see how color relates to our relationships and the raising of our children and explore the use of color in opening the intuitive and spiritual dimensions. In short, this book is a comprehensive study of the wide-ranging, practical, and effective uses of color, written so that you can learn the many ways to utilize the power of color, emotionally, physically, and spiritually.

RIGHT
The sun bathes the Earth continually with the light from which all color is born.

❶ Color and light waves

Light is a very small portion of the electromagnetic spectrum, which includes x-rays, radio and television waves, microwaves, and ultraviolet and infrared light waves. The waves move just like those on a body of water, except that these waves move in three dimensions and always in a straight line, radiating out in all directions from their source. We characterize electromagnetic waves by the distance between their crests. Some wave-crests are a meter or more apart, others, like gamma rays, are only billionths of a meter apart. Falling somewhere in the middle is the tiny group of waves we experience as visible light.

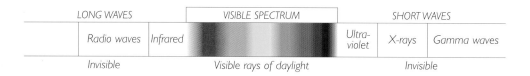

LONG WAVES		VISIBLE SPECTRUM		SHORT WAVES	
Radio waves	Infrared		Ultra-violet	X-rays	Gamma waves
Invisible		Visible rays of daylight		Invisible	

THE WAVELENGTHS OF visible light are very small, and units no more than a millionth of a millimeter are used—a millimeter itself being a thousandth of a meter or 0.03937 of an inch. The term for this tiny unit is an angstrom. Red light waves work out at 7,604 angstroms, or about ⅟₃₉,₀₀₀ of an inch. At the other end of the spectrum, violet waves measure 3,968 angstroms. In between is a continuation, without break, of all the wavelengths that make up the other spectrum colors. Given the width of the entire electromagnetic spectrum, there is relatively little difference between the two ends. Just off each end of the spectrum, and invisible to humans, are infrared and ultraviolet, which are visible to many other creatures like snakes and bees.

Life on our planet evolved within the narrow range of the spectrum to which we are sensitive. Other parts of the spectrum, such as microwaves on the longer side and x-rays on the shorter side, are dangerous, and can actually kill people and other lifeforms. The sun, our local source of almost all of the electromagnetic spectrum, emits vast amounts of many harmful waves. Our atmosphere screens them out, so we are protected. But when we damage it with pollution—in particular, ozone and fluorocarbons—we are ultimately harming ourselves.

Light waves travel at 186,000 miles per hour in a vacuum—as in outer space—but as they encounter denser material like air, or even denser material like glass, they slow down somewhat. When they change speed, they also change direction: they are bent. Because light of different wavelengths has a slightly differing energy, different light waves bend in slightly different directions. That is why when white light, which contains all the colors of the spectrum, enters the denser glass of a prism, the colors separate out into the colors of the spectrum.

Light also has many properties for us living on Earth, but its prime property as color is most significant. The human body is intimately keyed to color through its evolution. Our bodies and our very lives are linked to and exist because of the electromagnetic radiation we experience as color. Thus we can see why color therapy is an important method of treatment: it uses the very stuff that surrounds and governs our creation.

ABOVE
Visible light is only a small portion of the electromagnetic spectrum.

RIGHT
The slight energy difference in the various colors causes them to separate when passed through a prism.

History of Color Theory

THE THERAPEUTIC USE of color in its purely modern sense can be traced as far back as Hippocrates, who lived in the fourth century BCE. Referred to as the Father of Medicine, he used ointments and different colored plasters on wounds. Aristotle recommended the use of colored crystals, salves, minerals, and dyes as remedies around 300 BCE, and Aurelius Cornelius Celsus, the legendary physician of first-century Rome, used color extensively. But in the West, the coming of Christianity demanded that many of the ancient wisdoms were exorcised, and their practices deemed "pagan."

Few real advances occurred in color therapy until the Renaissance, when the superstitions of the Middle Ages began to bow before the newly discovered "science," which was finally able to move beyond Aristotle. During this period there was a great revival in the use of color – both decoratively and therapeutically—and in the ways in which people saw and described it. The oldest color terms were simply indications of whether a color was light or dark, or of its blackness or grayness. The new references were to colors, shades, and tints—the blueness of the sky, the greenness of a forest, the wine darkness of a flesh wound. At the same time, huge tapestries and murals were devised by sprinkling crushed minerals of different colors onto glue. The great physician of the Renaissance, Paracelsus (1493–1541), used color as a means of mental and physical healing, and was regarded as the most effective healer of his time.

The meanings commonly associated with various colors have evolved with time and experience. Many cultures have attached sacred meanings to color. The Aztecs and the Maya believed that each of the four directions of the compass had its associated color, and everything in their world was "colored" through them. Color was even offered as a gift to the gods, in the person of a young maiden adorned in colored feathers, her upper body red and her lower body yellow.

Today's understanding of color is rooted in the work of the renowned mathematician and scientist Sir Isaac

The Maya believed that each cardinal direction has its own color, expressed through the Mayan mystic cross.

Newton. In 1666 he passed light through a prism, and formulated a new theory: white light is itself made up of all the rainbow colors. It was Newton who first chose to divide light into the seven colors of the spectrum, equating them with the seven planets known at that time, and the seven notes of the diatonic scale. He considered light and color to be particles that moved in a straight line; his contemporary, Robert Hooke, believed them to be waves. It turns out that they were both right.

ABOVE
Sir Isaac Newton set in motion all of today's advance in color theory.

LEFT
Proper application of color can add life and energy to any environment.

Advances in medicine in the early 20th century led to scientific exploration into the healing aspects of color. Physician Dr. Dinshah P. Ghadiale began healing with different colored lights, calling his process spectro-chrome-metry—known as chromotherapy today. In 1903, the Danish physician Neils Finsen was awarded the Nobel prize for Medicine for his work on the use of light and color in healing disease. The most recent foundation of color therapy was laid in the middle of the 20th century by Faber Birren, in the United States, who brought together many diverse areas of color therapy and theory. Aside from the utilization of color as a therapy, it is widely used today in psychological testing. Dr. Max Luscher of Basel University has devised a simple yet effective diagnostic test based on color, used widely by psychologists, psychiatrists, and physicians. The medical profession makes extensive use of both infrared and ultraviolet light, and industrial psychologists are well aware of the effective use of color in the workplace. Even at this moment the history of color theory and therapy continues to unfold.

Man and Color

THERE IS SOME evidence that man's sensitivity and response to color has evolved over the ages. Recent linguistic studies have shown that man's development has a close parallel with the way in which color was perceived. In the earliest languages, linguistic studies suggest that there was little distinction between different colors—something was either "light" or it was "dark." The world was, in effect, colorless.

The first color for which a separate word was devised was "red." The color of blood appears to have had sacred meaning: in very early prehistoric burials the bones were disinterred, smeared with red ocher, and then reinterred. It was, perhaps, a gesture intended to return life to the deceased. Today in some Eastern European languages the word "red" is associated with life or beauty. The next colors for which separate words appeared were "green" and "yellow."

Yet still our color language is far from complete, even today. There are several languages being spoken at this moment that have no word for "brown." And, we have also lost certain color words: the Saxon word *wann*, for example, once described the gloss on a raven's wings, or the shimmer of moonlight on water.

Because mankind's development is so closely intertwined with color and color perception, it is possible to plot that development through the language of color, following the steps of the spectrum:

- **Cave man**—reproduction and physical survival—red
- **Development of agriculture**—complex toolmaking—orange
- **Domestication of animals**—yellow
- **Birth of civilization in Egypt**—the first cities/the first religious and moral thought—green
- **Growth of Greek philosophy**—blue
- **Reliance on law and civil order**—indigo
- **Sophistication and imperial grandeur**—the Pax Romana—purple
- **Renaissance**—the green of creativity
- **The Puritans**—gray morality
- **Industrial Revolution**—release from the shades of color
- **Space age/Aquarian age**—the blue spirit of truth

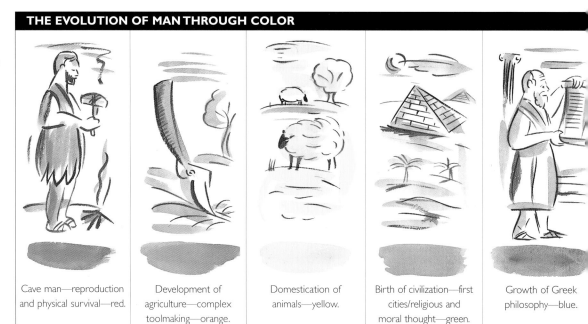

THE EVOLUTION OF MAN THROUGH COLOR

Cave man—reproduction and physical survival—red.

Development of agriculture—complex toolmaking—orange.

Domestication of animals—yellow.

Birth of civilization—first cities/religious and moral thought—green.

Growth of Greek philosophy—blue.

A LIFETIME OF COLOR

Human lifetimes can be monitored in phases of development using the seven spectrum colors of the rainbow as a growth chart. The chart below outlines each phase of development and the color that best represents that particular stage of life.

BIRTH TO 10 YEARS	●	**RED**	Physical expansion
10 TO 15 YEARS	●	**ORANGE**	Movement, dancing, athletics
15 TO 20 YEARS	●	**YELLOW**	Mental ability, education, study
20 TO 40 YEARS	●	**GREEN**	Relationships, love, children
40 TO 60 YEARS	●	**BLUE**	Transition from activity to contemplation
60 TO 70 YEARS	●	**INDIGO**	Perception—gathers together to make whole
70 PLUS	●	**PURPLE**	Visionary—no limitations

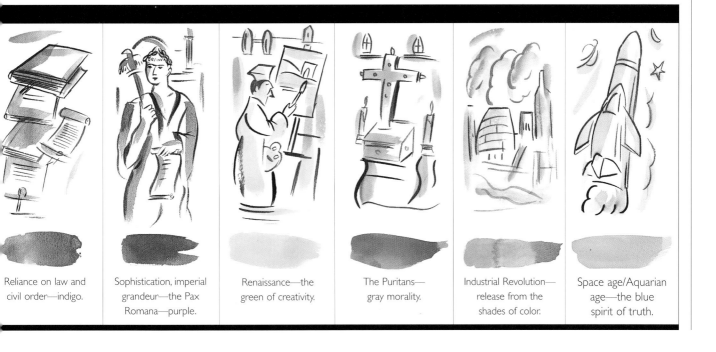

Reliance on law and civil order—indigo.

Sophistication, imperial grandeur—the Pax Romana—purple.

Renaissance—the green of creativity.

The Puritans—gray morality.

Industrial Revolution—release from the shades of color.

Space age/Aquarian age—the blue spirit of truth.

Shades, Tints, and Complementaries

WHEN WE TALK about color we usually refer to the hue, the single, definitive color, expressed scientifically by its diagnostic wavelength. Thus "red" is always 7,604 angstroms in wavelength. We now define color in scientific terms, but, as we saw in the pages on The History of Color Theory (see pages 10–11), there has been a great variation in the awareness and labeling of hues. Today we work from the basic seven spectrum colors—red, orange, yellow, green, blue, indigo, and purple—and further denote their shades and tints.

Tints are pale colors that have white in them, making them stronger for healing. For example, pale pink is surprisingly more powerful than the basic hue of red because of the abundance of white it contains.

Shades are darker colors; the basic hue mixed with black. All tones of a color share that color's basic qualities, but modified by whether they are a tint or a shade, lighter or darker than the original. Generally, tints are considered positive and shades negative; but the negative can be useful since it directs us to what we need to look at.

RIGHT
The hue of red, the pink tint of red, and the darker shade.

Hidden Colors

When working with color—particularly with healing—it is important to be aware of the hidden colors. For example, orange is made up of red and yellow. The eye sees orange, but the red and yellow energy that is within the orange will also be experienced by the body. When healing with orange, be aware of the red and yellow aspects, as well as the characteristics that relate to orange.

ABOVE
Be aware of the "hidden" colors when healing.

Green has hidden colors also: it has its own meaning, plus those of the yellow and blue that go into making it. Purple has red and blue within, so take note of these colors' attributes as well as purple's aspects. Gray is a mixture of black and white; likewise their meanings must be taken into account.

Scientists, industry, and artists have their own understanding of the working of color; however, when working with color as a therapeutic tool you must incorporate the psychological and spiritual meanings that are hidden within certain tints and shades.

Complementary Colors

Each color of the spectrum has an opposite color that complements it. Complementary colors are particularly helpful in healing, and they also find uses in everyday life. With them, you can pinpoint instantly the appropriate color for support and help.

When you are extremely irritated and feel furious at someone's behavior, at that moment you are reacting to an overload of the red energy within your system. The complementary color to red is the color blue, so visualize blue, put on some blue clothing, or focus on a blue object. Do this until the anger passes. Alternatively, you may find yourself in a room with a color that you find jarring. Perhaps a friend's yellow decor in the living room is unsettling. Rather than retreat, simply close your eyes and visualize purple, yellow's complementary color. This will dispel the vibration of the yellow, and you can enjoy your stay. Visualize, focus on, or wear the complementary to counteract the negative effects of a specific color.

BELOW

The complementary color chart.

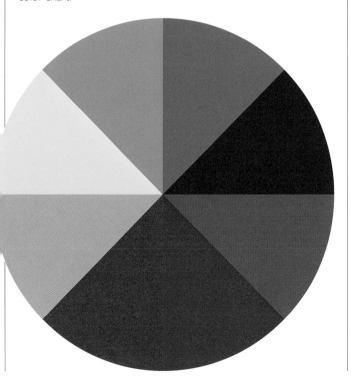

ABOVE

Bathe in green light to restore balance and harmony.

Complementaries can be of use when using colored light for healing—chromotherapy. A blue light can be used to relieve the red of irritability or, vice versa, use red light to pull you out of the blues. If you are in doubt about a color or feel that too much color has been used, flood the person with green colored light, or have them visualize it. Green acts as a neutralizer, bringing back balance and order to any situation. The complementary of orange is indigo and the complementary of green—the central color of the rainbow—is magenta, a mixture of red and blue.

2 The Psychology of Color

The human body is intimately keyed to color. Colors can be linked with our moods and states of mind. Reds, oranges, and yellows are warm and expansive, generating a feeling of energy, excitement, and joy. Blues, indigos, and purples are calming and cooling. The psychology of color is a language that can be learned, and when we understand its basic meanings we can interpret what color reveals to us.

THE STUDY OF COLOR psychology has been undertaken by eminent psychologists and psychiatrists. A leader among these was psychoneurologist Dr. Kurt Goldstein, a founder of Humanistic Psychology, who first came to prominence with his studies of brain-injured soldiers in World War II. When he turned his attention to color and its effects, he made a number of discoveries which underscored what color therapists and other color researchers had been working with for years. He found that colors affect the entire human organism, that each color has a role to play, and that a good balance of color was necessary for a healthy life. He confirmed the work of other researchers who had revealed that color response is deep-set, and intimately entwined with the entire life process.

From the standpoint of color psychology, Dr. Goldstein discovered that various mental conditions and psychological states have definite and varying responses to color. Other researchers have confirmed Goldstein's work, including Dr. Robert Ross of Stanford University, USA, who found certain colors were allied to dramatic intensity and strong emotion, and Dr. Maria Rickers-Ovsiankina, who confirmed even earlier work concerning the color preferences of introverts and extroverts. Color has also been shown to affect our sense of the passage of time, our sense of space, our senses of taste and smell, and it has been shown to be affected in turn by various sounds. Thus we can see that our entire organism is reactive to color, and its effects go beyond the immediate sensation. Because we are so interlinked with color, it is clear that the entire state of our being can be in some way represented by the colors we embody.

Because it is now widely recognized that a person's psychological state has profound implications on their physical state—that the two are, in fact, inseparable—color psychology is intimately intertwined with healing.

Using the Material in this Chapter

In the pages that follow, a number of colors, their shades, tints, and most common combinations are discussed. The colors are described in terms of their psychological meanings—which are also the meanings of the colors themselves—characteristics that will be referred back to at numerous points in the later chapters of the book. Read the characteristic as either personality or color appropriate, as necessary.

Each color's healing potential is also described, and this too will be referred back to in several places throughout the book. Use these color interpretations as necessary throughout the text, and remember that they are drawn from well-grounded scientific research, as well as the author's intuitive understanding gained through years of private practice. In a few places, you will need to use your own intuition to discover which interpretation or part of the interpretation is the correct one for you or others. It is part of the color-training process. Color is in many ways like a language: the more you practice it, the better you get.

RIGHT
Unusual sensitivity to color was one of man's earliest traits, still maintained by native peoples today.

Brilliance

BRILLIANCE IS THE clear, transparent, "original light" from whence all other colors spring, and return. Brilliance is not actually a color—brilliance should not be mistaken for white. It is not an earthly color: it is "cosmic light" that represents the Universal Intelligence. It is the clear light at the end of the tunnel that people report in near-death experiences—the clear light that *The Tibetan Book of The Dead* advises the newly deceased person to head for. . . All rays of color are brought into perfect balance through brilliance—it embodies the pure trinity of love, power, and wisdom. Our local source of brilliance is the sun.

Without brilliance there is no vision, either internally or externally. Brilliance cuts directly through to the truth; it is the hard light that exposes all flaws and corruption. Within brilliance is the essence of all qualities, both positive and negative, sparkling in their

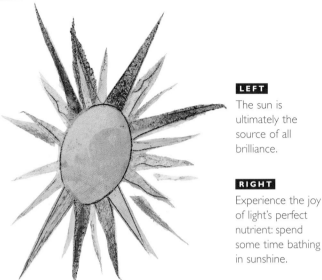

own perfection. When we say that a person is brilliant, we are acknowledging their purity of vision and the actions that arise from it. Brilliance is the pure Light that sustains our life. To say someone is "off-color" is literally true. We can sense that the person's light is muddied or diluted in some way. Should the light disappear entirely, the person dies. Where there is no light, there is no life.

Tints and Shades

Brilliance is the supreme light, so shades and tints are not identified. All colors come from brilliance, and it is to brilliance that they return.

Emotional Healing with Brilliance

Brilliance clears the way for necessary actions, and clears any cloudiness in a person or color. It brings hope when all seems lost. Situations become clearer because brilliance allows the delusions of our lives to dissolve. Using brilliance, we can maintain a balance between the world of restricting form—the material universe—and the formless "spirit" that everything emerges from and returns to. Brilliance promotes a balance between the heart and the head.

Brilliance is also the energy of transformation, embracing both the positive and negative within you, enabling you to wipe the slate clean and start again. It can bring about anything from a house move or a change of work, to a subtle transformation within. Old patterns will fall away to be replaced with joy and an uplifted spirit: a new you emerges. Crystal-clear brilliance will always show you the path as long as light springs eternally.

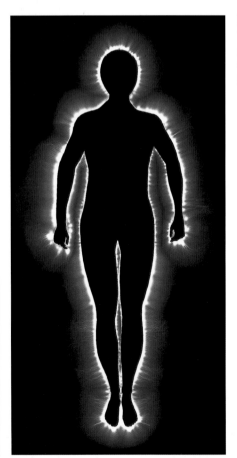

Physical Healing with Brilliance

Brilliance connects to the lymphatic system, and the areas that filter out the debris from our bodies. It is the unseen aura of life's energy force.

Many color therapists consider brilliance to be a "cure-all," with the power to modify any condition. But I always advise you to respect the clear, brilliant light, and use it sparingly for healing. Respect it as you would a burning fire. Brilliance can cause damage if used at random; however, a clean sweep of light, when monitored, can allow the body and mind to renew and start again. Brilliance is a great recharger.

The brilliant light brings about change, clearing away all that is unwanted. It acts as an antiseptic in the sickroom, removing bacteria and unpleasant odors. Exposing the body to a full-spectrum light in a darkened room can begin the process of clearing physical ailments, particularly allergies and chronic conditions. Open the curtains and let the power of sunlight enter the room and begin the healing process.

Light is a nutrient, and is vital for perfect health and well-being. We lack the brilliant light within our systems when we feel negative, lost, and alone. You can use a spectrum light bulb when you are confined to bed, or, if you are able to, take a walk. An equal amount of all the colors will penetrate your body, rejuvenating you at all levels. Drink plenty of pure water, which is liquid brilliance, to balance and bring tranquillity to the system.

White

WHITE CARRIES ALL OF the colors of the spectrum. Like brilliance, it contains equal amounts of each color. However, unlike brilliance, white has a density. If you hold a white sheet to the light you cannot see through it, whereas with brilliance you can. White's fundamental characteristic is equality: all colors are equal with white.

White personalities have faith derived from reason, and a tranquillity that conjures up hope. They embody fairness and unity and strive toward a purity of spirit. They do not discriminate, regarding all mankind as equal. White has an all-forgiving nature, even though it pursues the unearthing and exposing of all that is untrue. The white personality sheds light in dark corners. It has the ability to remove the blinkers so that the truth can be seen bringing about unity and harmony for all.

White personalities strive to save: you can be sure that all will be well when they are about. They are the ones who always show up in the nick of time: the white knight on his charger, the doctor in his white coat rescuing us from certain death, the cowboy hero wearing his white hat and riding a white horse. The white personality is efficient, if a little cold. Streamlined and precise professions suit them best and they always travel light. Banking, the civil service, and time-and-motion work fit the exactness of white; missionary work suits their deep faith, even unto death.

However, even white has its downside: while it conjures up hope on one side, on the other side its shade is its own worst enemy, leading to feelings of desolation.

Tints

White is the color that creates a tint when added to other colors, therefore there is no tint of white.

Shades

Shades are mixtures of black with another color, therefore, technically, white's shade is gray (see pages 46–47). However, white can also contain slight tinges of various other colors, and may then be described as "off-white."

White off-color can suggest that a person feels they have fallen from grace. They have suffered at the hands of inequality, which can be extremely frustrating. Isolation occurs and there is a feeling of emptiness, a barrenness of spirit.

RIGHT
White is the perfect color for professions that require precision.

LEFT
White light is composed of all the colors of the spectrum.

White Opposites
Fresh—Dirty

Positive White Keywords
❖ Unsullied ❖ Expansive
❖ Benevolent ❖ Truthful ❖ Peaceful

Negative White Keywords
❖ Secluded ❖ Bleak ❖ Harsh
❖ Failure ❖ Rigidity

LEFT
Meditate with white
for tranquillity and
purification.

Emotional Healing with White

White is useful for someone who has trouble opening up. It begins the process of cracking the ice, cutting through density, and removing the blinkers. For those who are rigid or have a one-track mind in some area, white gives them at least a small amount of each color. It acts to open the person to the whole spectrum of colors.

White encourages peace and purity. Place yourself in a white room when you need to restore your equilibrium, but do not stay too long as a sense of desolation may overtake the peaceful atmosphere.

White can also be worn as a general tonic, to top up all the colors in our body's system. White encourages growth and new ideas. It is the great opener that allows expansion and creativity.

Physical Healing with White

White does not distinguish one organ from another, in that it contains equal amounts of all the colors; however, the eyeball is connected to white, in that its shades of whiteness are used in diagnosis.

White is extremely good at keeping the lymphatic system clear. Visualize a white wash filling up the body and traveling around to clear the lymph sites, concentrating on the groin area, underarms, and the belly.

White helps to keep the skin lissom and moist. It is a lubricant that keeps the body supple, and, because it contains equal amounts of all the colors, it is a great tonic. White light wipes away and cleans, and is particularly beneficial for clearing bacteria in stagnant areas. White is also an antiseptic.

Red

THE RED CHARACTER is full of the spirit of physical life, the will to live. Red personalities are filled with adrenaline, determination, fire, and drive. Possessed of tireless energy, they embody courage, liberation, tenacity, passion, and excitement. The red character has a burning desire to get somewhere, but tends to act without thinking—it will get its own way, come what may. Quickening and exciting, yet practical, red makes a decision and gets on with it—no hanging about is acceptable. Red people are at best fine leaders of men, reformers and fighters, and builders of great things from very little. They are the explorers and pioneers, with the energy of the life-force at their command. Military and entrepreneurial leaders relate to red, especially where they combine strength with compassion.

Governor of sexual relationships, red, when aroused, will give a satisfying and passionate lovelife. Their zest for life and willingness to overcome obstacles makes them desirable, resulting in an exciting, long-term partnership.

Red Combinations

SCARLET, red tinged with yellow-orange, is a strange and dominating color that can be stronger than red. It creates a very pleasing, go-getting character—as long as it isn't crossed or opposed. The scarlet personality is very earthed, with great energy and drive, beneficial traits to have if you need to get a job done or start a campaign: it is a color that promotes pride in one's work. Love of life and enthusiasm are useful side effects.

CRIMSON, red with a touch of blue, has magnetic healing powers that give comfort in moderation, and it has the power to strengthen the individual. Emotionally it is much softer than pure red in its approach to life and its relationships, because of the blue aspect. Crimson highlights feminine beauty, combining intrigue with mystery. When their blood is up, crimson people are truly magnetic and persuasive.

FLAME is a fiery mixture of bright red and orange. It has the ability to sear through anything; it scorches and clears. Just like the hot poker used to cauterize wounds, flame color does the trick both mentally and physically, although it can be a bit harsh. Because there is some yellow in it, flame can act more quickly than some of the other reds, and has more mobility.

MAGENTA is a mix of red and purple, wielding the invisible energies of infrared and ultraviolet. The magenta personality accepts that "things are the way they are." They take the tender approach to getting what they want, and create achievement through love. They are the great arbiters, standing between antagonists to bring them to peace and a common understanding. Magentas know that if they wait long enough, they will get what they want. They are good at biding their time.

Tints

The pink tint is a higher vibration of red, because of the white infusion. Pink is known as the "great improver." It is unconditional love—love going out and love coming in—and is a good color to use in a crisis. Pink relieves depression and loneliness, comforting and mollifying. It is a powerful solvent, melting away anything unwanted.

If a young person is drawn to pale pink, it signifies that they are ready to develop their full potential, and they still have time to fulfil these expectations. If this color is chosen by an adult it is necessary to let go of unrealistic dreams and start to reassess, allowing one to get full reward from long effort.

ABOVE
Red characters like Sir Winston Churchill are fine leaders of men, strong and resolute.

RIGHT
Crimson highlights feminine beauty, emphasizing personal magnetism.

As pink becomes richer in color, there emerges a maturity, and a deep inner beauty that expands.

Pink represents spiritual beauty and upliftment, universal love, compassion, and the fulfillment of potential. Pink signifies the true love that we all search for, constant, faithful, and forgiving

Shades

The dark red shade is the downside of red; it signifies over-indulgence, brutal ambition, cruelty, and sexual excess. Inertia through hopelessness is a dark red trait. Dark red, at its worst, is tyrannical and murderous, seeking advancement no matter what, and oblivious to the suffering it may create in its headlong and headstrong rush. On the extreme side, perversity and bestiality can creep in.

Shades of scarlet indicate hindrance, a lack of scruples, and a manipulative organizer. The negative crimson is one who cracks the whip to make others work for their own ends. Shades of flame can cause you to leap before thinking whether it's right or wrong to do so. It can be experienced as a lick of fire that lashes the senses.

Dark red can appear too aggressive. Quarrelsome by nature, dark red characters must always win the argument. They can be full of guilt and shame, agonizing over what they have done to others. Equally, they can feel they have suffered a great deal themselves, resulting in feelings of sorrow from having been persecuted and abused.

Red Opposites
Expansion—Contraction

Positive Red Keywords
❖ Leader ❖ Resolute ❖ Fighter
❖ Vigor ❖ Diligence ❖ Esteem
❖ Reviver

Negative Red Keywords
❖ Brutal ❖ Lecherous ❖ Harsh
❖ Prejudiced ❖ Bully ❖ Stubborn
❖ Disreputable

Emotional Healing with Red

Red gives you a dynamic push that drives you on to achieve greater things, stimulating you and giving you the willpower to continue. It renews your enthusiasm to carry on. If there is something that you dread doing, or if you are feeling low or sluggish in any way, just apply a little red for support and quickening.

Red removes fear, and overcomes lingering and a reluctance to move forward. Therefore it is a good color to use to help someone face death, encouraging them to see their demise as the doorway to a new adventure.

ABOVE
Sensual red lips, nature's natural sexual signal.

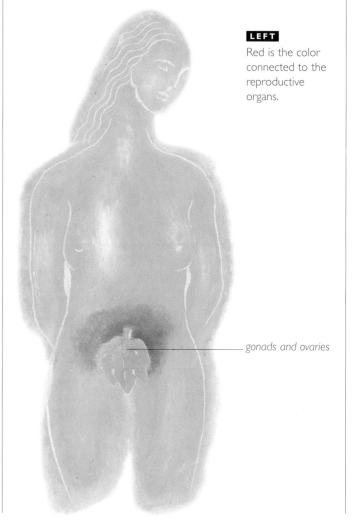

LEFT
Red is the color connected to the reproductive organs.

gonads and ovaries

Physical Healing with Red

Red in the body focuses primarily on the genitals and reproductive organs: the glands connected to red are the gonads and the ovaries. Another area of red focus is the blood and circulation: problems with red will show up as deposits clogging up the circulation or irregularities in the blood supply, blood clots, furring up of the arteries, heart attacks, strokes, anemia, and so on.

Red is a fiery force, eliminating negativity and the unwanted. It induces the release of adrenaline into the blood stream—hence its connection with overcoming aggression and fear, and increasing energy levels. Red eases stiff muscles and joints, particularly in the legs and feet. It is useful for paralysis, when combined with physiotherapy. Red is a real tonic for anyone who catches colds or chills easily. It is also a pungent detoxifier, and is notably good for freeing the blood flow. Magenta red has a beneficial effect on the entire endocrine system.

C A U T I O N

Always respect red while using it as a healer because of its potent energy force.

Do not use red lighting (chromotherapy) above the waist when treating heart conditions.
Professional advice should be taken for any heart problem.

BELOW
Always keep red light below the waist while working with any heart conditions.

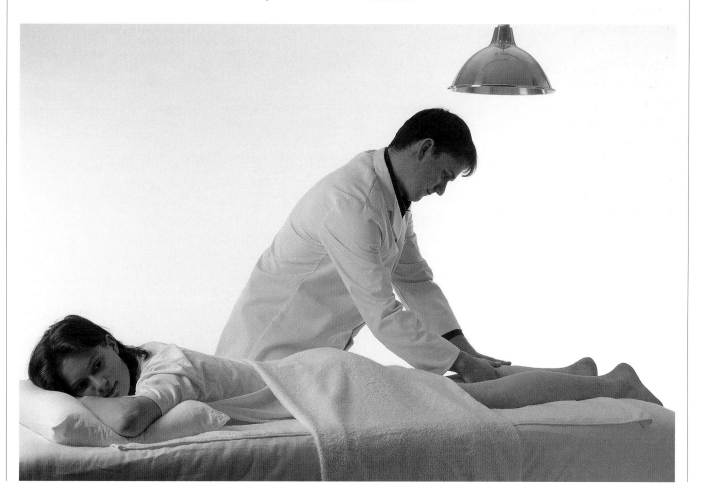

Orange

ORANGE PEOPLE ARE self-reliant, practical, genial, tolerant, benign, and warmhearted. Orange represents knowledge: it tests, and accepts or rejects. It has impetus, and persistence—but where red bullies, orange bides its time. Positive optimism is a particularly orange trait. The orange character is friendly, and may be the life and soul of the party. At the same time they are great supporters of the community. They like to work in groups, and can take pride in the achievement of the group rather than in their own success. Orange people are usually good cooks and sportsmen. The orange personality is warmhearted and generous, but at the same time it may be hindered by an inferiority complex.

Orange Combinations

CORAL Coral's personality challenge is to find its rightful place in this life. Coral characters are gentle souls, and always seem to be at the mercy of others. They are very willing people, but tend to be a little timid and sometimes need a helpful push. They love to socialize, but never seem to be in the right place at the right time. They are great listeners, and will help anyone in trouble. They possess razor-sharp minds, and they can severely chastise when they feel a wrong has been done.

AMBER The amber personality's presence is felt but not seen. They are good company but you may only be shown one side. They are very interested in others and what makes them tick, and they always seem to know just that something more than everybody else. They are single-minded, and have extreme powers of focus. They are open-minded and receptive, and have an innate sense of how the natural order of life works.

Tints

Peach personalities are the gentle persuaders. They feature the best qualities of orange, but without the impetus. Orange makes us jump: peach assures us it is safe to jump. Peach characters are good communicators, and they have an unusual talent for working with those teenagers who have no idea what they are going to do with the rest of their lives. The wise village elders are drawing on their peach aspects.

Shades

Dark orange personalities are the underminers, addicted gamblers, and inevitably have a chip on their shoulder. They are opportunists, but fail because they try too hard. Dark oranges often feel thwarted—misguided ambition is their major downfall and they seldom understand the reality of their potential (or, for that matter, lack of it).

The unkind practical joker is working from the negative dark orange.

Emotional Healing with Orange

Orange governs our gut instincts. It has subtle and gentle strength, and breaks down barriers. Orange can help in cases of mental breakdown,

RIGHT
The personality of orange shows itself in physical activity, making excellent sporting professionals.

FAR RIGHT
Orange removes inhibitions and psychological paralysis.

LEFT
The peach color gives us a gentle reminder that it's time to move on.

Orange Opposites

Activity—Indolence

Positive Orange Keywords

❖ Lavish ❖ Strong ❖ Unselfish

❖ Liberal ❖ Brave ❖ Genial ❖ Verve

❖ Sociable ❖ Fearless

Negative Orange Keywords

❖ Over-proud ❖ Gloomy ❖ Show-off

❖ Domineering ❖ Freeloader

❖ Deceptive ❖ Embarrassingly pushy

❖ Self-indulgent

depression, rape, divorce, and accidents. Orange is the most beneficial of all the colors for dealing with grief, bereavement, and loss. It is also useful when a person feels that they have been deeply outraged, bringing them up through the shock. Those who have a fear of moving forward in life because they cannot bury the past often dislike orange, yet orange is just the color to provide the strength they need to face such blocks. Its profound meaning is that all experiences, no matter how painful, have nutrients that we need. Amber helps one trust one's own judgement, and peach creates a safe environment for confronting difficult or painful memories.

Physical Healing with Orange

In its role of assimilator, orange is our intestinal laboratory. It is connected to the abdomen and the kidneys, and the lower back and lower intestines, and governs the adrenal glands. If the orange area of the body is out of sync, then the person will be unable to absorb any of the benefits of their life, whether physical or emotional.

Orange can aid with asthma and bronchitis, epilepsy and mental disorders, rheumatism, and torn ligaments and broken bones. It can be applied directly to limbs and muscles in physiotherapy. It is great for healing catarrh. Combine orange with yellow to treat the distress of menopause. Orange also balances the hormones for both sexes, and can aid with infertility problems.

RIGHT
Orange is connected to the intestines, lower abdomen, and kidneys, and governs the adrenals.

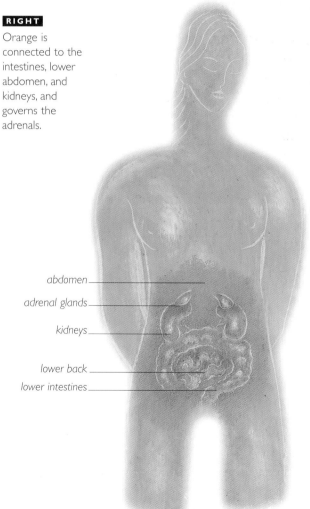

abdomen

adrenal glands

kidneys

lower back

lower intestines

Brown

BROWN REPRESENTS THE color of the earth and brown personalities are the very models of reliability and solidarity. They are the salt of the earth: down-to-earth, capable, and as safe as houses. There is not too much excitement about the brown personality, but there is a great deal of plain, common sense. Even so, despite the fact that they go about life with a quiet assurance, there is still a touch of the red fire in brown, which can surprise occasionally.

Being safe is a passion with brown people. They don't take chances—they have to be sure before acting. Until then, they hold their own counsel. Browns are slow but sure developers. Deep thinking and studious, they understand that there is more to life than one can see. The person embodying the brown vibration can fathom out where things went wrong: they have remarkable depths of single-minded concentration.

ABOVE
Coppery bronze represents quiet and effective activity. It brings about changes without dramatic displays.

Those under the influence of brown can be an effective right-hand man or woman. They will hold the fort while you are away without plotting to take over your position, and will relinquish it gladly when you return.

LEFT
Brown is the "salt of the earth," reminding us of nature's ability to continually recycle.

Brown Combinations

COPPERY BRONZE Those who relate to the coppery bronze side of brown are quiet but effective in whatever activity they undertake. Because it contains several colors within it, bronze represents multiple positive aspects. Flow and balance are two words particularly associated with bronze personalities. Bronze activates the understandings that allow personal change to take place without drama.

TAN Those who relate to tan show a quiet assurance, and deep intuition. They have an intuitive trust in the natural order of things on earth. They check every inch of the way, making sure that the ground is firm before they make their move.

Tints

Beige is a soft tint of brown and beige personalities have a softness about them, and are single-minded, with a stable affection that is utterly reliable. Creamy beige personalities help others to come to terms with reality, giving an assurance that it will all turn out right in the end. They like to establish a firm foundation, yet are open to taking a risk in order to protect their brood and their own patch. Beiges like to be rewarded fairly for their work, but may find it difficult to get what's due to them. The aspect of intuition is clear with this tint, and those who operate from it know clearly what's what.

Shades

Dark brown features the negative features of the brown personality. Dark brown people are self-centered and biased—dark brown is associated with selfishness of all kinds—and care nothing for anyone else's opinion. This often prevents them from seeing the wood for the trees. Stubbornness can be another major hurdle because they are sticklers for doing it "right," which often results in not doing anything at all. Dark browns are traditionalist to the extent of missing out on the best of the new. They can also be emotionally hindered because of a reluctance to face tomorrow.

Brown Opposites		
Accumulation—Decay		
Positive Brown Keywords		
❖ Solidarity	❖ Reliability	
❖ Moderation	❖ Sobriety	
❖ Caring	❖ Confident	❖ Loyal
Negative Brown Keywords		
❖ Self-doubt	❖ Withdrawal	
❖ Frustration	❖ Discontentment	
❖ Desolate		
❖ Obsession with decay		

Emotional Healing with Brown

Because of brown's soothing capabilities, it allows us to snuggle up to the bosom of Mother Nature. Because it is close to the earth, it can provide a cloak of security and earthy support during times of emotional storm and stress. A highly therapeutic way of working with brown is, of course, in the garden—particularly turning the earth over and planting. Those suffering from the downside of brown need to stand up and show their true colors once in a while.

Physical Healing with Brown

Brown, like white, gray, and black, is not specifically connected to any parts or organs in the body. Brown's physical function within the body is to make us aware of elimination. When Mother Nature calls, it is brown's reminder that the recycling of all life continues.

ABOVE
The brown husks of seeds guard the powerful life-force contained within. Brown promises potential.

Yellow

YELLOW PEOPLE ARE mind-oriented, precise, optimistic, clear, and in control through the intellect. The yellow personality is one of focused attention, yet at the same time it is flexible and adaptable, and a lover of new ideas. Scientists function through their cerebral yellow aspect. This dimension unravels and reveals, leaving no stone unturned. The counselor also relates to this color.

Yellow people have quick reflexes, both physically and mentally. They never have any hesitation; they decide instantly, and act immediately.

Yellow is the color of the "great communicators." Journalists and media people—press, radio, television, and entertainment—all embody yellow. They are people with no shortage of words.

Yellows are sunny and willing, unless upset, when they can become acid and sharp-tongued. People feel good around yellows, who are always full of fun and broadcast a general feeling of well-being.

Yellow people are big thinkers when it comes to money, even to the point of flamboyance.

Finally, those under the influence of yellow exhibit style and sophistication. Broad-minded by nature, yellow personalities loathe pettiness.

Yellow Combinations

LEMON yellow people are very practical and astute. No one can pull the wool over their eyes. They prefer to cut through the verbiage and red tape, and just say what is what—which is not always the most popular line. They often gain a reputation for being critical and suspicious, but at the same time, their perceptiveness can be an asset.

YELLOW-RED Those people who relate to yellow-red may, at their best, express the wonderful healing power of mercy. But there is a problem. The red in this color highlights a tendency to rashness and impetuosity. Yellow's justice may turn into a harshness, where the punishment far outweighs the crime.

CITRINE yellow's personality can be summed up in one word: fickle. Their emotions are unstable, and often conflicting. They can be foolish about money—and are most likely to be the fool who is soon parted from it. They can be deceitful, and watch for deceit in others.

LEFT
Primrose-yellow subtly exudes its spiritual grace.

RIGHT
Lemon yellow reinforces
practicality and astuteness.

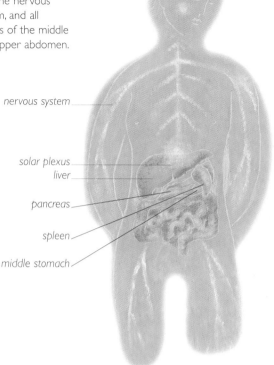

RIGHT
Yellow is the color
relating to digestion,
skin, the nervous
system, and all
organs of the middle
and upper abdomen.

nervous system

solar plexus
liver

pancreas

spleen

middle stomach

They can be coquettish
and teasing. Their redeeming
feature is that they are
discriminating, and have the
positive aspect of fairness.

Tints

Yellow's primrose tint represents those who stretch their
minds, and question the world beyond the obvious.
They search for meaning and deep understanding.
Primrose yellow personalities may have a great
spirituality, but it can be an erratic devotion. There may
also be a tendency to drop out, so that they can spend
their time pursuing life's unanswerable questions. Gifted
children relate to primrose, however.

Shades

Dark yellow people exhibit low self-worth and
misplaced confidence. They are crafty, treacherous, and
argumentative. They exemplify the fact that you can fes-
ter in the mind just as you can in the body. Dark yellow
personalities expect the worst of others, and themselves.
As they embody the darker mustard yellow shades, the
negative traits deteriorate even further. They regard
honor as stupidity, and are total cynics. Dark yellows are
overly analytical, often making them
nagging, complaining, and caustic.

Emotional Healing
with Yellow

Yellow is an excellent color to use
against depression and melancholia.
Anything that adversely affects the solar
plexus, or reveals itself by changes in that
area, is likely to benefit from yellow.
Yellow usually brings to the surface that
which the person most needs to look at,
and gets them talking. Mentally, yellow

clears away woolliness and negative thinking. Emotionally,
it boosts low self-esteem, encourages joy and laughter, and
is particularly useful for releasing fears and phobias.

Physical Healing with Yellow

Yellow is connected to the pancreas, the solar plexus,
liver, gall bladder, spleen, digestive system, middle stomach, and to the skin and nervous system. Yellow is excellent for ridding the body of toxins, and
it stimulates the flow of gastric juices,
toning and cleansing the system. It is a
stimulant for the lymphatic system, and
is good for menopausal hot flashes and
for menstrual difficulties.

Yellow is used for clearing congestive
conditions and constipation, and is also
useful for ear problems, skin rashes, and
abrasions. Some have found that yellow
also offers relief from the symptoms
associated with diabetes, rheumatism,
and anorexia.

Yellow Opposites

Discernment—Evasion

Positive Yellow Keywords

❖ Quickness ❖ Mental deftness

❖ Unprejudiced ❖ Original

❖ Incisive ❖ Honest ❖ Just

Negative Yellow Keywords

❖ Cynical ❖ Faithless

❖ Self-preoccupation ❖ Superficial

❖ Hasty ❖ Condemning ❖ Vague

Gold

GOLD PERSONALITIES HAVE a purity that speaks simply: I am. They do not seek, because they have already found. They have access to deep inner knowledge, to their own soul experience from all that's past. Most importantly, they know themselves. Gold is the wise old sage, who understands that wisdom is given to be handed on to others, not to be hoarded for oneself. They are extremely gracious, and believe in honor among men. They absorb facts quickly, and are superb advisers, always knowing what is needed.

Gold is also a color of leadership— leaders always have a golden streak within, a depth of self-knowledge that puts them in front. Gold people are certainly nobody's fool.

Gold is the color of experience and maturity. Gold spent years underground, maturing, and when it is dug up, it represents solidified sunlight. The gold personality is never young. It has weathered the trials of life and has a treasure trove of old memories.

Gold Opposites

Faith—Doubt

Positive Gold Keywords

❖ Maturity ❖ Enlightenment

❖ Abundance ❖ Tolerance

❖ Achievement ❖ Success

Negative Gold Keywords

❖ Cynicism ❖ Mistrust

❖ Obstructive ❖ Sullen ❖ Misfit

❖ Ignorance

Tints

The only way you can acquire the pale gold halo of sainthood is through the genuine experience of self-denial. The sweet tears of humiliation that come with pure pale gold are from the understanding of insignificance, and yet at the same time a deep respect for the magnificence of that obscurity. Pale gold has always paid its dues.

LEFT
The pure color gold is like its metal: solid, incorruptible, and represents triumph.

RIGHT
The highest wisdoms and the truths that endure the ages belong to gold.

Shades

The darker side of the gold personality is measured in conceit: yellow's conceit is trivial compared to that of negative gold. Dark gold personalities never hesitate to blow their own trumpet, and their belief in their own inherent superior worthiness is unparalleled. Privilege is thought to be theirs by right. Like fool's gold, they are filled with unreal expectations. Deep down they are very fearful, and trust no one. Dark gold people are forever chasing the key to eternal youth to the extent of missing out on today.

Emotional Healing with Gold

The golden tears of forgiveness are the greatest healer of all—the forgiveness and letting go of the past that arises out of a deeper understanding. Gold's gift is released because it expands the power of love through trust. When you trust you can surrender, and when you surrender, you can receive. Gold is very uplifting for both physical and psychological depressions, and it dissipates suicidal tendencies. Vitality and abundance flow from gold's attribute of endless supply. Whatever appears to have been lost or taken away will return.

Physical Healing with Gold

There are no parts of the body connected to gold, which is an offshoot of yellow, but it can be seen in some auras.

Gold soothes the nerves, and bestows an overall feeling of well-being. Gold means "I am"—it helps one to come to terms with what is. Thus it is good for depression during the menopause, which is based on a reluctance to let go of the menstrual pattern, and a feeling of being worthless as a female. Likewise, it also has a useful role during male menopause.

Physically, gold is good for digestive irregularities, irritable bowel syndrome, rheumatics, and underactive thyroids. It is also beneficial for rashes and skin irritations. Since gold won't allow anything to cling to it, it shakes off any kind of parasite—emotional as well as physical—anything that is not really part of you.

Green

GREEN IS POSITIONED midway between yellow and blue: it is a bridge, the gateway in the spectrum—just as the heart is in the body. To cross green's bridge, the lesson of love must first be learned.

An idealist, green has a strong social conscience. Green people are often quick to help others, even when this is at their own expense. The green character is dependable, diplomatic, and tactful. Greens would rather be admired than loved, and they can tend to put themselves on a moral pedestal. The search for balance, harmony, stability, and a settled way of life are particularly green traits. Clarity and understanding are at green's core: a green person can see both sides of any argument. Although green personalities can experience a conflict of ideas and emotions, causing commotion and upheaval, paired with their ability to discriminate and balance, this conflict can ultimately lead to the correct judgment and action. Green people want to take their proper place in life, and want to be acknowledged for being who they are, and not what they own materially.

LEFT
Dark green reinforces the physical constitution by detoxifying the system.

Greens are often prosperous, particularly in business. They like the "good life," and love to collect possessions; yet at the same time they are generous and love to share what they accumulate. They are the givers and servers of mankind, loving children and animals. Greens like to be seen as deserving: many doctors are "green" people. A love of outdoor work is another green characteristic, and they make excellent farmers and conservationists.

Green Combinations

EMERALD green embodies the highest qualities of charity, tolerance, and adaptability, and is the color that particularly manifests itself in great healers. The emerald green ability to go to the heart of the matter assures that heartfelt choices succeed without struggle. Emerald green people have an abundance of wealth—in ideas as well as materially. There is a grandfatherly or grandmotherly air about them that is comforting, and instils a sense of security.

GREEN-GOLD Those whose character embraces green with gold become the automatic supplier, with a knack of producing whatever is needed as the moment demands. It is a real "can get" and "can do" personality, bringing the confidence of gold and the calmness of green together. Green-gold personalities are always in the right place at the right time. They have the connections, and come up with the goods. A perfect green-gold career is buying for a large store.

GREEN-BLUE people can be trusted with your deepest secrets—confidentiality is their byword. They are capable of the true giving of self from the heart, and they have the ability to keep quiet about another's affairs—of the heart or otherwise. Those who relate to the green-blue combination show compassion and understanding for others, which is one of their best traits. The confidant and the priest in confession are acting from the

green-blue part of themselves. There is a worldly wisdom about them, and space for psychic knowledge.

LIME GREEN introduces acidic yellow into green and creates a sharpness in the personality. Lime adds a kick to everything it encounters. This color will need a regular work schedule, welcoming challenges and advancement. The process of propelling themselves into new directions creates escape routes for others—but they will hire someone else to take care of the details.

Tints

Tints of pale green represent fresh starts, forever young and expectant. The pale green character is the person who is always at the "beginning" of something new—possibly even a new and exciting phase of their life. Pale greens are inspired, the idealists who are kind and gentle. They love to take part in fresh projects and adventures, and they are forever looking forward to new romances. Pale green people can show considerable sympathy and compassion for others, but at the same time they can also express indecisiveness and immaturity because of their inexperience.

Not willing to admit or act one's age is a pale green trait. Peter Pan, for example, was a pale green character. Adults who are uncomfortable with pale green can be indicating childhood deprivation, where a sweet child's innocence was dashed before its time.

Shades

As green darkens, there is an increasing tendency to resentment, extreme possessiveness, and blindness to the needs, wishes, and emotions of others.

Everything is supposed to revolve around the dark green person. Self-deception, envy, and animosity are pitfalls. Someone under the influence of this color can be unreliable, and lack imagination.

Those people who relate to dark green have often been misdirected children, whose aspirations were once smothered. The result is emotional resistance, subsequently manifesting itself in a physical equivalent: rheumatism. It can also show that the person is full of remorse and despair or can resort to greed and avarice.

Emotional Healing with Green

Green is made of two primary colors, yellow and blue, which, when combined as green, help bring to the surface that which needs to be resolved. Yellow is the color of clearing up and blue is a bringer of insight. This makes green a very important healing color, in that most of our physical and psychological illnesses result from events and conditions from our past. Green's characteristics of clarity and understanding come to the fore here. Its power to stabilize helps to reestablish balance, and restores and brings ease to the system.

Applied during stormy periods in a relationship, green will calm and cool the emotions. Because it gives direction, it can be used when you are trying to make up your mind or heart—it brings everything back into focus.

Green is a sanctuary—the halfway house of the spectrum.

Green-gold is useful for nervous tics and stammering, and for anyone suffering from a severe neurosis, and green-blue is helpful for manic depressives.

Physical Healing with Green

Green is connected to the thymus gland, heart, shoulders and chest, and to the lower lungs.

Green is good for shock and fatigue. It helps nausea, soothes headaches, and is beneficial in cases of claustrophobia. It

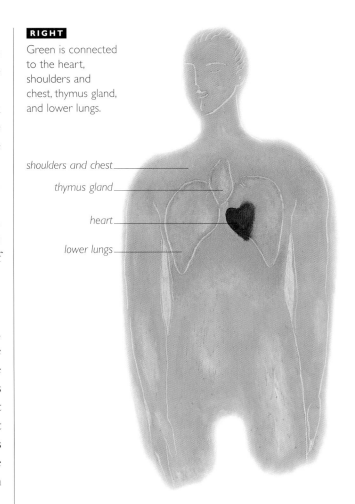

shoulders and chest

thymus gland

heart

lower lungs

restores stability to anything malignant, lowering the overstimulation which results from cells that have accelerated out of control.

Green is the greatest nerve tonic. It can relieve head colds and hay fever. It is a particularly effective aid for complaints of the liver because it is such a good detoxifier. Green is wonderful for nausea or upset stomachs, especially when on holiday when a change in diet occurs. It can even help with malaria.

Green-blue is a good aid for the heart, whether it be on an emotional or physical level.

Green Opposites
Balanced—Unstable
Positive Green Keywords
❖ Judicious ❖ Sensible ❖ Fruitful
❖ Benevolent ❖ Magnanimous
❖ Talented
Negative Green Keywords
❖ Suspicious ❖ Resentful
❖ Unmindful ❖ Grasping
❖ Banal ❖ Unreliable
❖ Disappointed

Turquoise

TURQUOISE IS THE only color that allows the personality to concentrate solely on the self, instead of everything and everyone. The turquoise personality appears extremely calm, and very balanced, but there is a fire burning beneath that cool exterior. Turquoise people say what they feel rather than what is appropriate. They have a very discriminating eye because they are exquisitely perceptive. They are lovers of antiques and usually acquire some bargains. They are very self-sufficient, and when they want to be, extremely ambitious.

Turquoise personalities are inclined to dither when making a choice of partner, and can become involved with two people at the same time. Turquoise is a very human color, bringing in the love of sharing, and always striving for compatibility in work, play, and relationships. The turquoise person's basic motivation in life is personal relationships; they are the best friends you can have. They love family life and hate being single—togetherness with a partner is the goal of the turquoise character. They also have a great rapport with animals.

Tints

Pale turquoise people crave enjoyment from life. They are inclined to be romantics, and to concentrate obsessively on acquiring that single mate—the love of their lives—which they are certain will bring them utopia. Their working life can suffer as a result, since nothing really interrupts their search for personal romance and love. They can possess extreme charm and are lively lovers; their soul mate must be sensual as well as spiritual.

Shades

Dark turquoise can be cold and aloof, but in an effort to communicate may actually appear boastful and unreliable. Dark turquoise people are emotional controllers *par excellence*. They are easily self-deceived and waste unnecessary time waiting for

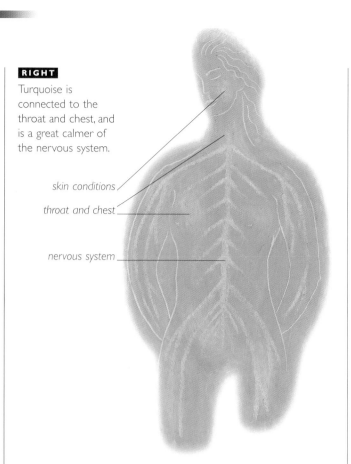

RIGHT
Turquoise is connected to the throat and chest, and is a great calmer of the nervous system.

skin conditions

throat and chest

nervous system

that perfect partner that never comes. The dark turquoise personality is narcissistic by nature, but will wither and collapse if their object of desire leaves them.

Emotional Healing with Turquoise

Turquoise can work rather slowly as a healer, but persistence definitely pays as it will get there in the end. It is a particularly good healer for the emotions and pains of the heart, and is instrumental in straightening out affairs of the heart. Turquoise is also excellent for

Turquoise Opposites
Sociable—Withdrawn
Positive Turquoise Keywords
❖ Calm ❖ Introspective ❖ Self-sufficient ❖ Self-possession
Negative Turquoise Keywords
❖ Reticent ❖ Indecisive ❖ Boastful ❖ Undependable ❖ Deceptive ❖ Narcissistic

ABOVE
Carry a turquoise-colored stone to bring deep inner peace through the stillness of its color.

encouraging self-questioning and releasing from confusion. Turquoise is the only color that allows you to think of yourself first, instead of your partner. It is the perfect comforter for anyone who feels alone and unlovable. It is also a great support to those who have suffered nervous breakdowns caused through entangled love affairs. Turquoise can help in overcoming self-sabotage and can restore confidence to the downhearted.

Physical Healing with Turquoise

In the human body, turquoise is connected to the throat and chest. It is also a great soother and healer of the nervous system. It is helpful for minor skin rashes, insect bites, and other skin problems, and also for light fevers

and infections. Turquoise can help with the growth of new cells, particularly with scalds and burns—but always seek medical attention first. Exposing scars to turquoise helps them to fade. Neuralgia and all conditions pertaining to the teeth and jaw can also benefit from turquoise application.

Turquoise is also useful for all age-related conditions, such as those droops produced by the law of gravity! It is a reliable rejuvenator.

Blue

BLUE PERSONALITIES EMBODY the saying "still waters run deep." Blue is the color of the higher order of intelligence; it is the "spirit of truth." The throat is blue's domain, and both the head and the heart speak through it in people relating to blue's aspect. They are deep thinkers and won't leap without much forethought.

Blues possess a tranquil spirit, yet it is peace with a purpose: their thinking is quiet and discriminating. Integrity, honor, and sincerity are blue traits. There is a poise about blue people, but they will not seek attention themselves. They are highly inventive, and are often drawn to poetry, philosophy, and writing as professions.

Blue Combinations

SKY blue people have an unusual capacity for selfless love. They remain calm in a crisis and can overcome all obstacles. Like the sky, they are changeable, but there is an underlying constancy that always brings them back to their own perfect inner reality.

AZURE blue people are filled with ambition. The waiting period is over for them. The struggle may have been hard, but now they are finally free to take up what is rightfully theirs. Azure blues reach for high spiritual attainment, for the stars themselves. Under this color's influence, they have found what they want and are going all out to get it and make the most of it.

Tints

Pale blue people are inspired. They have constant faith and the purity of innocence. They are the souls searching for spiritual maturity. They are constantly struggling upward toward a purpose; they are those in whom the spark of ambition is catching alight. The great spiritual healers reside here. However, they can also do a lot of work with little to show for it, and there is sometimes a tendency to miss opportunities.

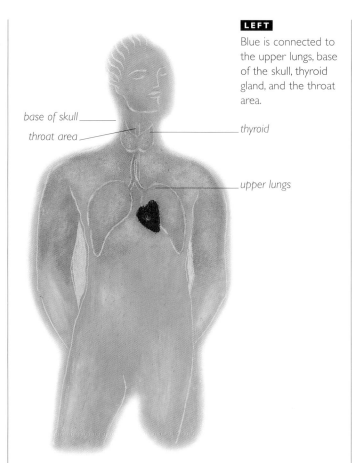

base of skull

throat area

thyroid

upper lungs

Shades

Dark blue people exhibit a single-mindedness that can be used to good or not-so-good ends. The black in this shade indicates a restriction and a hardness that inclines them to justice without mercy. They are often dissatisfied with their lot, and they can have a rather gloomy disposition Where blue has intuitive gifts, in dark blue it can become the charlatan. Dark blues are not noted for their honesty. They are masters of manipulation. They are so good that you may not even know you have been manipulated! They don't like upsets, yet they often cause them.

Emotional Healing with Blue

Peaceful blue brings rest; it cools and calms. It is useful for looking back onto one's past: it takes a person back to

Blue Opposites
Wisdom—Stupidity
Positive Blue Keywords
❖ Serenity ❖ Sacred ❖ Peaceful
❖ Reflective ❖ Faithful
Negative Blue Keywords
❖ Feeble ❖ Malevolent
❖ Emotionally unbalanced
❖ Unfeeling ❖ Dishonest
❖ Ruthless

rituals that mark their family's identity. Blue combats the fear of going forward. Stiff necks, often representing this fear, can benefit from the application of blue.

Blue can help those who need to learn the power of the spoken word—not so much to help others but to help themselves; to understand that what you don't ask for you rarely get.

Physical Healing with Blue

The glands related to blue are the thyroid and parathyroids. Blue is also connected to the throat area, the upper lungs and arms, and the base of the skull. Infections in the throat area are often psychologically related to not speaking out and blue can help in such instances.

Blue is a beneficial color for treating children's ailments, such as teething, and ear, throat, and speech and vocal problems. It can also be useful for incontinence at any age.

Flood the sickroom with blue light because it cools and calms, and it is particularly useful for the terminally ill and in reducing fevers and inflammations. Blue relaxes you, and helps you to allay your fears.

ABOVE
The blue of azurite reaches for the stars, releasing itself from bondage.

LEFT
Blue in all its glory creates freedom of spirit.

Indigo

THE INDIGO PERSONALITY is forceful and powerful, with a devotion to truth. For indigos it is all or nothing—there are no in-betweens. They are pure thinkers, and reverence is second nature to them. They can see beyond the obvious and they plumb hidden depths. Indigo people are the aspirants to spiritual mastery, and have a genius for reconciling science and religion.

The indigo personality loves rituals of any kind, but they need to remember that a ritual is only a preparation for our intent, and it is wise to keep in mind what the original intent was. Indigo can get caught up in the preparation, forgetting that a preparation is only a reminder of the path.

Inspired preachers, writers, and actors are drawing on their indigo dimension. The indigo personality can be dramatic and intoxicating—although, on the sexual level, they can be Casanovas or *femmes fatales*.

The acting profession provided an outlet for the dramatic antics of Errol Flynn.

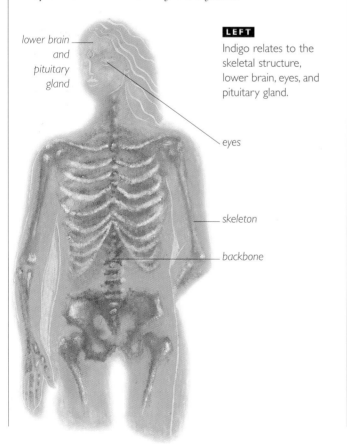

lower brain and pituitary gland

LEFT
Indigo relates to the skeletal structure, lower brain, eyes, and pituitary gland.

eyes

skeleton

backbone

Indigos are all about structure. Terror for indigo is the absence of form or direction, or any area in life that shows a lack of focus. Their inner vision allows them to see through the illusions of the material world, but it leaves them lost in space. To anchor themselves, they create structures in which no deviation is considered either possible or desirable, often drawing on or maintaining ancient ways in the process. They are great promoters of justice and peace—lawyers relate to this color.

On the down side, an indigo characteristic can mean bigotry and fanaticism. Blind devotion to people, causes, or ideals is an indigo failing. All addictions relate to the negative of indigo, in that they are rooted in the failure of life's structures.

Tints and Shades
The depth of color of indigo means that tints and shades are not identified.

Emotional Healing with Indigo

Use indigo when you need a push into reviewing your thinking because it is the color of knowing. It has a sense of when to move energy and when to hold fast. Thus it helps gather together what is necessary at all levels, and making the whole that allows the journey toward somewhere else to begin. Indigo prepares you for the realm of mystery and psychic dimensions—a color of spiritual opening. It is the color that looks beyond the immediate complaint and gets to the structural cause of the trouble. It is the great healer of painful memories, and is a good cleanser and purger, cleaning away addictive emotional ties. Indigo helps the emotionally shattered to regain direction in their lives. It can reveal the hidden fears that are concealed in the indigo sea of darkness.

Physical Healing with Indigo

Indigo connects to the skeleton, and in particular to the back-bone. Its gland is the pituitary, which is the most complex of the glandular system producing hormones that control many functions throughout the body. Indigo also relates to the lower brain, the eyes, and the sinuses.

Indigo is the most powerful painkiller in the spectrum. With its ability to transmute and purify, it can clear up bacteria and the results of air, water, and food pollution. It can be used to help bring down high blood pressure, and is particularly effective at treating an overactive thyroid. Many other complaints respond to indigo, including lumbago and sciatica, migraine, eczema and inflammations, chest and lung complaints, bronchitis, and asthma.

Indigo is also good for acute sinus problems, which, psychologically, are often connected to uncried tears from childhood. This color is the best antidote for insomnia and is helpful for controlling diarrhea. Indigo can aid with any kidney complaints and disperses growths, tumors, and lumps of any kind. It is also a good healing color to steady anyone who may be suffering from drug, alcohol, or abuse of any kind.

Indigo Opposites
Devout—Faithless
Positive Indigo Keywords
❖ Discrimination ❖ Organization
❖ Conformity ❖ Tenacity ❖ Purification
❖ Compliance ❖ Obedience
Negative Indigo Keywords
❖ Addiction ❖ Authoritarian
❖ Overpowering ❖ Puritanical

LEFT
Indigo is the threshold to other spheres. It helps you enter new realms.

Black

BLACK IS CONNECTED to our higher philosophical thoughts and ideals. Out of the black come all new ideas and new beginnings. Within black is found every color of the rainbow; black therefore holds the mystery of hidden colors. Unlocking the black personality reveals all the person's hidden talents.

We all have within us a light and a dark side. The black side is not necessarily the negative, since in a positive vein it represents mystery, visionary ability, and the mystic secrets. Within the black personality lies something dormant or buried, just as the black of winter contains the seeds for the next spring. At the heart of black lies discipline, which in turn brings about freedom and liberation. Any cause that gives genuine support to and works toward the light is working with the strength of black. Black positively embodied is the dark earth out of which all new life springs.

But when the opposite side of black is embraced, the worst aspects of the will and power come forth: harsh behavior, treachery, and deceit. Those relating to the negative side of black can believe that all is ended, that there is nothing to look forward to, and they fear what's coming next. Thus, it may show that a person has a need to be in control, in order to allay their fears. One of the ways black personalities keep control is by not giving information to others. There is nothing weak about black's character, they are quite capable of overcoming extreme restrictions, and will even self-flagellate to achieve a state of unhindered purity.

Tints and Shades

Because of the depth of color in black, shades and tints are not identified.

Emotional Healing with Black

No color can be labeled as either "good" or "bad." Even the negative aspects of black can be used positively: it shows the way. Sometimes we need to destroy the old and habitual in order for the new, fresh, and innovative to come into our lives. The black of night holds the promise of rest from our daily battle to survive: we retreat within black to rest and wake into the light again. Black is perfect for those needing to be on hold while disturbances are sorted out. It allows a "stand still" period to occur. This is particularly useful for treating addictions of all kinds because it provides the space to investigate new options. But remember that a little black goes a long way—overdoing it will cause regression instead of progression.

Someone who takes to wearing black continuously may be saying that there is something absent from their life. Depression is the greatest challenge of black. It is

LEFT
The positive embodiment of black is in those who seek their own deep inner mysteries.

The unique black sheen of a raven's wing had its own special name in Old English: *wann*.

what they cannot face that keeps a person in the black, it becomes like the womb, a safe and hidden place in the world just for them. Introduce other colors into the daily life of a black personality as quickly as possible.

Physical Healing with Black

There are no parts of the body that are specifically connected to black, except when they are seen on x-rays or in the aura as disease.

When black appears consistently, either seen in the aura or chosen as a color for interpretation, it indicates that a close look at the person's physical habits is necessary. Bad habits, such as staying up late at night, leading to sleep deprivation, can eventually cause physical illness. A little of indigo's discipline is required

Black Opposites
Promise—Nothingness

Positive Black Keywords
❖ Right use of strength ❖ Artistic
❖ Idealist ❖ Unseen wealth

Negative Black Keywords
❖ Wrong use of strength
❖ Difficult ❖ Superiority
❖ Despair ❖ Restraint

The black of obsidian is the visionary color of higher philosophical thoughts.

here to encourage the right behavior. Black brings order out of chaos, and a completeness to the incomplete. It will put on hold anyone who is over- or hyperactive—wear black clothes three days a week until stability has returned.

Gray

GRAY IS THE BRIDGE between black and white, the point where innocence and ignorance meet. At its best, the gray personality is optimistic, and knows that the best is yet to come. At its weakest, it believes it cannot have what it wants today, but might get it tomorrow. Unfortunately, tomorrow never comes. The gray personality is always desperate to leave their present situation. Grays feel they are never first, that it's always someone else's turn. They also fear their own lack of definition.

To be described as "gray" has tended to mean dull, yet gray's tenacity is as firm as a rock, constantly striving for a harmonious stability. Gray people will never rush into a project or falsely commit to any situation. Always ready to offer a helping hand, they usually do the jobs that no one else wants to do. They prefer to live a quiet, respectable life so that they can have space.

Tints

Those who relate to the light gray tint are the rescuers and bringers of salvation. They battle against all odds, and are able to count their blessings even when they may appear few. Light grays embody a higher vibration of gray, because this tint has more white in it. They seek the light that will enable them to adapt and move on. Great peace of mind and tranquillity are characteristics of this tint, yet the light gray person can feel as if they don't belong—light gray often indicates the beginning or end of a journey.

Shades

Dark gray personalities are conventional to the point of narrow-mindedness. It is the shade of suffering and poverty, and thus of shame and humiliation. Tortured minds relate to dark gray, always trying to escape from some unknown anxiety. They feel trapped, that there is no way of escape. They are often struck by melancholy. Old age and frailty is

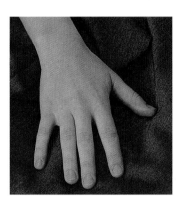

constantly in the back of dark gray's mind. Dark gray personalities always manage to leave a blemish, wherever they are involved. But, their behavior is bizarre rather than insane.

Emotional Healing with Gray

Gray is a color for stabilizing the disturbed. It can help one to break free from the chains that bind. Light gray is a restorer of sanity and a blocker of deception. It can be used profitably to sober up someone who is utterly reckless and irresponsible. A preoccupation with a fear of death and dying can be indicated by gray, the color of breakdown. This shows that the person's inner light has become dim, causing malaise.

Physical Healing with Gray

There are no body parts connected specifically to gray, but when gray appears it represents breakdown. Gray suggests trouble is brewing. It is the only color that gives prior warning of ailments and illnesses that are about to manifest. Gray should be used as an indicator that the body is in urgent need of attention, and to review one's care for the physical self. Regard the gray color as an x-ray, showing hidden parts. It is principally a tool rather than a healer. When the skin and nails have a gray tint, it is an indicator of congestion somewhere in the body. Use orange as an antidote, particularly for any thick mucus in the sinuses, chest, stomach, or bowels.

Gray Opposites
Positive—Negative
Positive Gray Keywords
❖ Well-versed ❖ Sane
❖ Genuine ❖ Reputable
❖ Spartan ❖ Soothing
❖ Seer of spirits and ghosts
Negative Gray Keywords
❖ Destitution ❖ Illness
❖ Dispirited ❖ Fault-finding
❖ Misery ❖ Depression
❖ Restless ❖ Unattached

Silver

THE SILVER PERSONALITY can be summed up in the phrase "still waters run even deeper than blue colors." There is a constant yearning in silver people for spiritual harmony—silver is the thread of cosmic intelligence. Silver characters have quick, penetrating minds, are unbiased, and allow others to have their own opinions, without the need to try to change them. Silvers never stand about—they are constantly changing like the waxing and waning of the moon. Silver's lives always remain in a fluid state. They are lovers of the sea and all tidal movements. Professions that create make-believe work are under silver's influence. Of course there is a downside. The "let's pretend" side of the silver personality shows up in relationships where there is illusion with no substance. Those who fall in love with stars of the "silver screen" clearly exhibit this aspect.

These personalities can have a quicksilver temperament, becoming very slippery, tricky characters. They can be elusive and have a very odd attitude toward society and its workings. Silver's least attractive aspect finds it difficult to get a grip on what actually is the point: indecisiveness is another trait of this side of silver. Schizophrenics operate on the negative side of silver, but silver personalities also have the ability to be powerful reflectors, mirroring back the truth to those around them.

Silver does have the quality of endurance—even out of sight the silver personality is never out of your mind. Instead, they keep returning to shine brightly within your orbit. Temperamental by nature, silver personalities have star-quality and natural glamor, and always appear gorgeous however they are attired. They love to fantasize and can be fun to have around—their yarns will enthral you. There is also an elusive magic about the silver character, an urgency about the persona that stems from a deep understanding that tomorrow they may be gone!

Tints and Shades

The presence of brilliance in silver means that tints and shades are not identified.

Emotional Healing with Silver

An invisible silver cord is said to attach us to the spirit realm. At death, the cord is severed and we move on. The spirit is able to travel in meditation along the silver cord to glimpse the infinite. It reflects and illuminates.

Silver is the great natural emotional tranquilizer. It stills the emotions and restores equilibrium. It can absorb negativity, setting a person free from restraints. Silver reflects our past mistakes without distortion, apology, or bias: a mirror never lies. Silver illuminates and pierces, it lights up the path. It penetrates and lays bare that which we need to face. Our greatest teaching and learning come from our mistakes. Silver can show that a person is full of illusion, living a life that doesn't really exist, and reflects distortions so that corrections can be made.

Silver Opposites
Increase—Decrease
Positive Silver Keywords
❖ Reveals ❖ Contemplates
❖ Unbiased ❖ Astute ❖ Flowing
❖ Reflecting
Negative Silver Keywords
❖ Deceitful ❖ Disconnected
❖ Slippery ❖ Inauthentic
❖ Split personality

Physical Healing with Silver

There are no body parts specifically connected to silver. The feminine part of the self is represented by silver, whether in a male or female body.

Silver helps calm the nerves as well as settling the hormones. It brings about a fluid, harmonious state of consciousness. Saturate yourself with moonlight to restore your equilibrium. Silver calms the system and allows the physical and mental functions to flow freely.

Purple

PURPLE REPRESENTS THOSE operating on the Royal Ray. Within their domains, purple people are the rulers. Spiritual mastery is also under purple: those who strive for enlightened perfection do so under its influence. Also found here are the visionaries, working with the highest levels of thought, and seeing and hearing without using the physical senses. Those under purple use its psychic perception on an everyday basis.

The purple personalities are the great teachers. They realize that the pupil has to understand that facts and figures alone are not enough. Clergymen, gifted poets, writers, painters, and musicians, in fact, the masters in any creative field, are all associated with this color. Purple people are humanitarians who are both wise and humble—but their kindness is never mistaken for weakness. Purple personality traits are of gentleness with power; combining the two is the challenge. They are not generally good mixers in public, although they abound with delightful charm. Purples are not happy being employees, and are more likely to be self-employed. A positive use for purple is to let it help bring out your leadership qualities.

Those who embody purple come to understand that the price they must pay for their leading role in life is sacrifice. But they can sacrifice themselves for the benefit of others without being martyrs. Their humility is a key aspect in their successes.

Purple Combinations

VIOLET is the color of those in spiritual service. They have many of the attributes of purple, but they are not so intense. Violet people work from intuition, rather than intellect. They can see into the future and seem to receive divine inspiration because of a touch of the brilliance within violet. Violet personalities can be very idealistic, and they adore to revere. They are usually outstanding in their life work, but do not adjust well to a decline in their circumstances. Violet is a very good color to use for past life regression work.

AMETHYST people are those deeply in touch with their mystical powers. Amethyst has both crimson and blue within it, thus idealism is its key. The crimson aspect earths, while the blue uplifts at the same time. Amethyst

LEFT

Purple always works along traditional lines.

RIGHT

The lavender color is not as delicate as it seems. It probes deeply into the mind, transmuting negativity into love and beauty.

people are likely to become the protectors of those who are unable to protect themselves—small children, the sick and vulnerable, and animals. Monks and missionaries relate to this color: their amethyst vibration sends them out to the unknown to guide and help mankind. Those working from amethyst go beyond the calculated reasoning, and easily assess who is sincere and who is not.

PLUM contains purple and rich gold. Its people are the people who have arrived—they experience no struggle to achieve and attain because they are already there. They have the majesty of the privileged who know their circumstances and take full advantage of the knowledge. A plum person could be the inspiring schoolteacher that the child never forgets. However, plum people must be cautious of falling

Purple Opposites
Composure—Animosity
Positive Purple Keywords
❖ Leadership ❖ Altruistic ❖ Dignified
❖ Humane ❖ Artistic ❖ Boundless
❖ Spiritual leader
Negative Purple Keywords
❖ Merciless ❖ Spiritual haughtiness
❖ Self-important ❖ Base ❖ Social snob
❖ Megalomaniac

in love with their own publicity, and developing false pride and a holier-than-thou attitude.

LILAC personalities are rarely lacking in self-appreciation; but, it can turn into vanity—either too much or too little. There is nothing wrong in glancing in a mirror, but not at every one that you pass. Lilac people love glamor, romance, and magic. Lilac in the character can also reveal a lost childhood; growing up too soon. Lilac people may exhibit a degree of immaturity and adolescence, but they may also possess great healing powers.

Tints

The pale purple tint of lavender tends to be delicate and sensitive by nature, and lavender personalities can be elusive. That elusiveness may mask another characteristic of lavender: the iron butterfly—delicate on the outside, but strong underneath. Light lavenders love beautiful things—a collector of exquisite porcelain is operating from the lavender. They have a light disposition, gaily tripping through life, having a good time. Yet they possess a deep understanding of destiny for themselves and for others. Lavender indicates the highest form of dedication to spiritual work, and lavender personalities have an uncanny ability to perform psychic readings, connecting to anything associated with the past.

Shades

Dark purples can be belligerent and treacherous. The negative purple traits are accentuated by the black within that allows dark purples to use their power corruptly. Overbearing and very arrogant, dark purples can become ruthless seekers of power, and may have delusions of grandeur. They may find themselves dedicated to an ideal at the expense of human reality, locked in dogmatism. Romantically, they can be inclined to marry for position rather than love.

Misinformed mystics can be found here too. Wrapped in impractical ideals, cults built upon brainwashing techniques operate on the downside of purple.

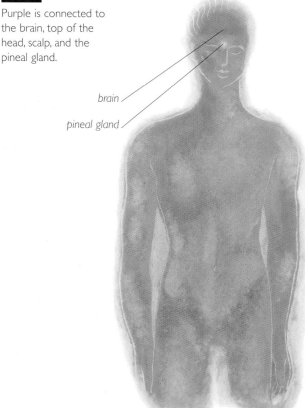

RIGHT
Purple is connected to the brain, top of the head, scalp, and the pineal gland.

brain

pineal gland

Emotional Healing with Purple

Purple, being made of red and blue, has the body of red and the spiritual nature of blue held in perfect union. It is the bridge to higher planes of consciousness, the springboard to the infinite. This color brings relief to all mental illnesses. Violet is useful in regression work to acknowledge your inner child, or your inner child from other lives. Lavender is a great aid for assisting the person who desires to delve into their physic ability. It is also a great healer for all excessive emotional disorders.

Physical Healing with Purple

Physically, purple represents the top of the head, the crown, the brain, the scalp, as well as the pineal gland.

Given the cautions expressed above, purple is a very useful color. The color purple activates the pineal gland and it can be used to increase spiritual awareness. It relaxes all the muscles, including the heart, and is thus good for palpitations. Purple is good for internal inflammation, disturbances of the immune system, jangled nerves, and severe headaches. Purple is an extremely beneficial color for head-related problems such as scalp conditions, shingles, concussion, and all conditions appertaining to the brain. It is likewise a good color to slow down overactive kidneys. Purple releases menstrual pain, and

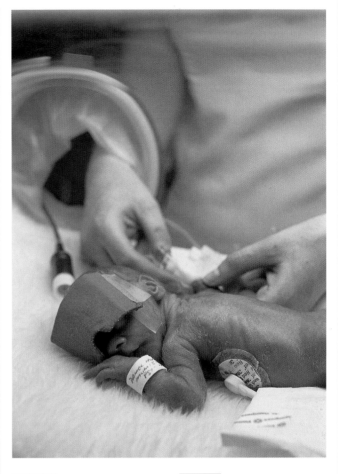

BELOW
The purple plum doesn't have to strive to attain. It already has what it needs.

ABOVE
Violet light has been found helpful in eliminating jaundice in the newborn.

removes pressure and sensitivity to pain. It also decreases bleeding and hemorrhaging.

Because of violet's link to the unborn child, it is useful for treating infertility. It can also help with the pain of neuralgia and acute inflammation of the nerves, and it can be used to treat eye complaints.

Lilac has great healing powers and strengthens the immune system. Lavender is the color of convalescence. It works on the brain's pain centers, thus helping with drug addiction, and is also useful for clearing anesthetics from the system.

③ Color in the Environment

Color and its messages lead us into all realms of the universe. Color is there for the taking, and what better way is there to harness its mysteries, benefits, and strengths than to use it to enhance our environment at home, work, and play? Light and color are crucial to our health and well-being; nature and her colors have the answers, and by learning her lessons we can continue the power and presence of color in our own environment.

WE KNOW THAT virtually all of our senses are influenced in some way by color. It can lift our spirits or depress us; it can speed us up or slow us down; it can soothe or it can irritate. We also have sufficient knowledge of the effects of color to enable us to plan and apply it to achieve a specific effect.

Our "environment" is literally all that surrounds us at each and every moment, awake or asleep. Even simple things such as changing a baby's blanket from a stimulating color to a soothing color will affect their sleep. Changing wall colors at home can change the mood – and, indeed, the habitability – of a room. Color in the workplace can have a dramatic effect on the whole working environment. One of the greatest post-war revolutions in color technology has been its application on the factory floor. Not only has it provided an improved atmosphere, but there have also been unexpected spin-offs, such as improved worker morale and, more significantly, a massive improvement in safety. One factory in the United Kingdom found that their accident rate dropped by three-quarters within a year of introducing a factory-wide color scheme. The specific application of color to the workplace has become possible only in the past few decades, when paints have become available that are durable enough for industrial applications, and their color range wide enough to have useful effects.

The safety aspect is not limited to the factory floor. Color consultants have been instrumental in creating safety colors for children's, walkers', and cyclists' clothing that stand out against the gray, brown, and buff streets in poor lighting conditions. Color consultants have revolutionized hospitals, clinics, and other places where healing is focused, through the use of appropriate colors. In psychology, great strides have been made in the diagnosis and treatment of certain mental conditions through color, and tests of color preference have been created that reveal personal attributes useful in determining where a person's talents may be most successfully applied.

The use of color in its many possibilities is both an art and a science. The color consultant combines knowledge, intuition, and judgement. These are talents we all possess, and the information and exercises in the remainder of this book are directed to helping you develop those talents within yourself.

Color is a tool. As such, it requires practice to develop the skills you need to use it properly. But first and above all it *is* a tool, and the skills of its use are available to all who make the effort.

New names for colors are constantly being invented, and color names often change to suit the requirements of commerce. For example, one paint company renamed the color of one of its products, and successfully boosted sales that had fallen under the old name. Different countries call the same color by different names, creating problems when ordering or producing products in the international market. Thus the color world is still a place of growth and new discovery, and the opportunities to positively influence the environment grow proportionately.

RIGHT
Colors in the environment send powerful messages and condition our responses.

Enhancing the Mood of Your Home

HIGHLY SATISFACTORY RESULTS can be obtained in interior decor provided the necessary care has been taken to use the appropriate color, instead of choosing haphazardly. Use color as a cosmic tuning fork and it can create tranquillity and harmony. Poor color schemes can shock the eyes and cause discomfort and fatigue, but, with a little time and care, color can be used in the home to produce an atmosphere of comfort, joy, and happiness.

Your personality is the key to your choice of decor, so bear this in mind when making decisions. A quiet person using stimulating colors because it seems the done thing will have difficulty living in their own home, and you should never choose a color scheme because it's fashionable—ultimately you have to live with it.

The room's size and shape are also important considerations. Strong colors close in on a small room, making it claustrophobic, but if decorated in single, light colors, small rooms look spacious. Dark, narrow rooms in particular need light, clear colors. Colors also become more intense in larger rooms than in small.

Dark colors can look good with the sun on them, but they will be several shades duller at night under electric light. At the other end of the scale, check how much daylight a room gets before using white, because an overdose of white can be tiring for the eyes and cause frustration. Beige can be used virtually anywhere, but add a strong color or two—no more than two—to give a boundary to beige's expansiveness. When painting one wall in a different color, do not do so on a wall with a door or window since this dissipates the color energy. A dark ceiling or carpet shortens the walls, while pale colors open a room up. The strong, expansive colors of red, orange, and yellow will have an immediate impact upon the eye and make the space. The contra-active colors of blue, indigo, and purple quieten energies, cooling and calming any interior. As a general rule, keep all the hot colors—reds, oranges, and yellows—downstairs, and use the cooler colors—from blues to purples—for bedrooms and bathrooms upstairs.

The Living Room

When planning the decor for the living room, it is important to consider color as more than just pleasing to the eye. Color enables you to stamp your own indelible mark, but the effect color has on the people who use the area must also be taken into account. In this busy family area, each individual can express themselves, so it is vital that you choose colors that suit you and your family's widest needs. By selecting the correct color and surrounding the occupants with that color's vibration, you can influence the room, thwarting disturbing activity like arguments. Those prone to quarreling need a nice, rich blue in the room. If you like to have family gatherings or friends to visit, then choose yellow walls to loosen the tongue, keep the conversation flowing, and encourage fun and laughter. A strong green in the living room will aid digestion after moving from the dining area, but do not have everything in this room green, because too much exposure to green creates a soporific atmosphere and eventually leads to depression.

LEFT.
The yellow in this room brings in joy and fun encouraged by the beige sofa, promoting expansion of space.

ABOVE

Blues in any home environment will always cool and calm the atmosphere, promoting peace and relaxation.

RIGHT

The pewter-gray color of a stainless steel work surface in the kitchen will restore sanity and tranquillity to a busy place.

The Dining Room

Restaurants have discovered that the most food is eaten when the decor includes white and brown. The brown links physically to nature—the brown earth where food grows. White is connected to mother—mother's milk, the original source of nourishment and comfort. These two colors fare well together, allowing the digestion to work well under brown's steady influence. Add a touch of turquoise to the decor, or through plates, glasses, napkins, or flowers to encourage genial conversation. You can always bring in other colors to suit: blue, indigo, and purple for a dinner to be lingered over, and red, orange, and yellow to speed up the proceedings.

The Kitchen

The kitchen is a busy place, so it is not the best area to use blues or purples in, since these have a slowing-down effect, just when you need to get busy. Yellow is a wonderful color for the kitchen because it stimulates the intellect, helping you to concentrate on the job at hand. Terra-cotta and orange are also perfect because they promote action and activity. Bright green in the kitchen encourages wonderfully healthy food to be conjured up. Use red sparingly in the kitchen, however, as it tends to encourage an exit from the place of work, which will not help the person who doesn't like cooking. Red can also become claustrophobic in a confined space.

The Entrance Hallway

The entrance decor gives visitors the first indication of your personality and home environment. The warmer the colors—such as corals and peaches—the more welcoming they are. A good color to feed the nervous system is turquoise; add a touch of blue for calmness. A yellow hall shows that the family would like to keep you there talking, rather than taking you through to the rest of the house. Green halls show that the family may not be too tidy, as they usually have a love of the outside as well as animals. White and blue suggest that the occupants are very creative and that the design and effect of their homes are important to them. There are usually no children in this household, but there may be a Siamese cat eyeing you up! A brown hallway allows you to enter, but you won't be staying.

The Basement

Basements can be dark, dank, and dreary, with little light. The best color to use in them is white, because it is reflective and will widen and lighten the surroundings. If there are pipes surrounding the walls, paint these with all the colors of the rainbow, making them a splendid feature instead of an ugly eyesore. Also paint cupboards or any odd shapes with exquisite bright colors, so that they sing out to you in fun and joy.

ABOVE
Three perfect colors to offset stark white or beige walls in any room.

Bedroom

A bedroom is a place of rest, so decorate it with all the blues, plus lavender, lilac, and violet. Red and orange in the bedroom tend to be too stimulating, and can cause sleeplessness. Indigo is a good color to use for insomnia, and indigo in the bedroom is also great if you suffer from migraine or headaches. A little gold can be introduced to allow the occupant to surrender to a good night's restful bliss. Use different-colored light bulbs, night attire, and colored sheets for different moods. Removable red ornaments or roses can be used to revive a slow sex life.

LEFT
The purple carpet protects the home environment. The occupants will be totally aware of their social standing.

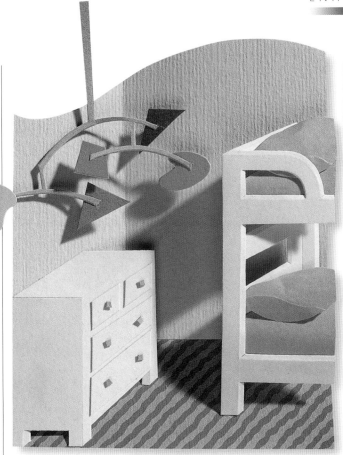

Incorporate both ends of the spectrum
in an infant's room.

The Children's Bedroom

Keep it simple. Too many colors overwhelm, and will keep a child awake. Children's bedrooms need both ends of the spectrum present among the walls, carpet, or furnishings. A cool, pale apple green is appropriate, as usually the child has different-colored toys to bring in the extra colors. The older child studying for exams benefits from primrose yellow walls, to encourage and help the intellect to concentrate on the work at hand. Yellow also encourages a flow of energy, so the child does not feel bogged down with too much work. For advice on nurseries, see pages 82–87.

The Bathroom

The bathroom is the room we go to in order to detoxify, cleanse, and refresh ourselves, ready to start all over again. Water is a great healer, so use your bathroom as your own personal sanctuary from the stresses and strains of modern life. Use bath salts or bubble bath that

turn the water turquoise, enabling you to concentrate on yourself at this precious time. Use dark green plants to detoxify the body, along with dark green or yellow candles. An exotic bird-of-paradise bathroom encompassing all the colors of the rainbow and, using jungle-printed paper or tiles depicting butterflies, birds, and flowers, can be a real haven. To avoid overload, incorporate plain white to provide some much-needed breathing space. A blue bathroom with sea shells can encourage relaxation, as well as creating the sense of swimming in healing waters. Hot colors in the bathroom do not invite you to linger, which could make them a good choice for busy families whose time is limited.

A plain white bathroom can be used with colored lights or accessories for specific healing, such as orange light for the alleviation of rheumatoid arthritis, or indigo towels to relieve a hangover. Refer to Chapter 2 for color-healing suggestions.

Hot colors in a bathroom make them a good choice for busy families whose bathroom time is limited.

The Healing Garden

THE UNIVERSE IS full of color, and we can harness her bounty to enhance our lives. When we stroll in our parks or gardens, we are nearer to God's love than anywhere. We can design our gardens specifically for healing. The blue sky already reflects on earth the color that signifies the healer. The green of grass has tremendous qualities for strengthening the physical body and can detoxify a clogged-up system. Trees with their brown trunks remind us of the dark depth of the earth's potential, with bounteous colored fruits nestling in the tree's green leaves. To sit under a tree is to connect to nature's healing force. Embrace a tree or gently rub your spine up and down its bark to generate nature's life energy.

Dark gray paving stones, cement, or concrete can restrict a garden's healing energy, so it is better to use terra-cotta bricks, multicolored stone, or natural wood, which all blend in with the outdoor surroundings and boost natural color energies.

Winter Color

Become aware of the changing seasons in your garden. Nature provides unlimited colors throughout summer, and can also do so in winter. Yellow flowers, such as winter jasmine and furry catkins, add a ray of sunshine to a bleak cold day, and winter colors can also be found in bright red, orange, and yellow berries.

When a garden appears barren, why not lay clusters of colored crystals or stones on the lawn or in the flower beds, or even hang them from bare stems and bushes to provide some much-needed color energy. Paint the dull garden shed yellow, or gold and white. Garden benches can also be painted in wonderful colors to suit your needs. A splendid orange to encourage the spirits and warm the heart and soul would stand out wonderfully against the background of dormant brown earth. Orange also encourages the production of vitamin C within the system. Brightly colored flowerpots in all the colors of the rainbow lined up on a window ledge will promote healing every time you see them. A kaleidoscope of color can be visible in the garden, even when the sky is gloomy and gray. The ground covered with snow is redirecting in equal balance all the colors of the rainbow.

Vegetables

Since the beginning of time, the sun has been bathing the earth with its glorious rays: nature's warm red and gold thermal colors have an expansive effect on vegetables and the insect world. Each colored vegetable has its own vibrational rate. Different-colored vegetables can add another color dimension to the garden, and are a good way of putting the colors we need into the body to improve and maintain health (see pages 104–105).

Herbs

You can also introduce sunlight's balanced spectral colors to your body by eating herbs. Green herbs represent circulation and the bloodstream of the vegetation world. Green is produced in nature by the sun's rays manufacturing chlorophyll, and it is a great boost to the system as a health tonic.

RIGHT
The soft cream of an ornamental cabbage in a window box compensates for the lack of space.

RIGHT
Flame red flowers add a promise of zest and energy to any garden.

Flower Power

Flowers represent a material show of light. Since ancient times they have been used as symbols of healing and examples of beauty and love, and to represent the present and the future. Love is the criteria for healing.

Plants and flowers may not have a central nervous system, but scientists are proving that their cells have extrasensory perception: polygraphs connected to plants have shown that their tracings match, beat for beat, the pulsating heart rhythms of their owners. It has been suggested that plants are capable of transferring life-giving energy. Somehow they even seem to speak to each other. That is perhaps why the golden marigold is considered to be the doctor in the garden—not only are they extremely sensitive but are physic as well!

Utilize the power of color in flowers for everyday use. The flowers you take to someone in hospital are extremely important. Do not take oranges and reds if the person has just had an operation and needs rest, blue and green are better. In the workplace, sitting at a computer,

ABOVE
A floral healing bath is a particularly beautiful way to infuse color.

ABOVE
Lilac-colored flowers have great healing powers for strengthening the immune system.

a purple African violet, placed on the machine or nearby, would be perfect for counteracting any negative rays.

Healing Flower Tinctures

Bach flower remedies, discovered by Dr. Edward Bach, are safe, complementary remedies that can be used on their own or with other treatments. They are aimed at the emotional body rather than the physical and bring the mental state into balance, allowing the "divine will of the soul" to encourage healing.

FLORAL HEALING BATH

You can use flowers as a particularly beautiful instrument for infusing color. Caress a blossom in your hands, then transfer your hands and the blossom into water. The bloom will infuse the bath with color energy. You can also add the perfume fragrance of flowers to water for extra healing power.

The gathering of flowers brings in love. In folklore, flowers were regarded as the ever-perfect blossoms from spirit, which could be placed in the garden of your heart. Choose any colored blooms that are appropriate, and only use fresh flowers. Drooping flowers infuse the bath with declining energy. If you wish to relieve pain, blue or indigo flowers are ideal. To lift depression, use a profusion of golden yellow petals. Pink flowers are perfect for consistency of unconditional love.

Flower Symbols

Flowers represent the feminine principle and are said to evoke paradise—an eastern word meaning "walled garden." Many people who have had near-death experiences bring back the memory of a colorful "healing garden." The colors of the flowers are particularly remarked upon, being described as "vivid and exquisite."

- The cup is the center and represents receptiveness.
- Buds signify potential.
- Open flowers represent expansion, the wheel of good fortune.
- A basket of flowers symbolizes longevity and a happy old age.
- Flower seeds embody the rebirth of the spirit.

Shrubs

A lovely, subtle way to introduce color into the garden is to include shrubs in variegated colors. Shrubs are usually everlasting, and are much prized for their glossy, strong foliage, rather than for their flowers. A group of shrubs in various shades of green gives off a tremendous aura of healing, bringing a balance to the system. Use a combination of light green and dark, along with shrubs that have variegated leaves that feature green tints and shades. A purple-leafed shrub planted among the green gives the most beneficial color combination there is. Combined, they promote color balance with celestial wisdom and spiritual growth. Yellow-leafed shrubs provide a dash of excitement, because yellow is the brightest color of all.

BELOW
The variegated colors of shrubs bring a mixture of shades and tints to the garden.

Enhancing the Mood of Your Office

THE CORRECT USE of color in offices has emerged as a vital means of comfort for employees, and increased productivity for business. Equally, it is important to be aware that improperly applied color can interfere with and distract from work.

Color is an effective means of changing the dynamics of a room:

1. Single, light colors make small rooms look spacious.
2. Dark colors enclose a room.
3. Strong colors also enclose a room, causing claustrophobia.
4. Colors are more intense in larger areas than small.
5. Darker ceilings shorten the walls; pale ceilings open up a room.

Colors to Avoid

On the whole, it is best to avoid white offices. White contains all colors, so there is very little direction from it; it tends to create irritability with long exposure, reducing productivity. Brown is also a poor color: it creates tiredness and stagnation, a closing-up of energies. Gray colors produce melancholy and black restricts movement, keeping everything on hold. If beige is used, add green or rose to alleviate the slackness that too much beige can bring.

Colors to Use in Specific Settings

An important consideration is the purpose of the office. Is it intended to be a place of creative contemplation, or full of the buzz of free-wheeling high finance? Secondly, what effect is desired? To boost energy, or to relax tension? To focus on a single item, or to support wide-ranging lateral thinking?

THE EXECUTIVE OFFICE

Executive offices need to convey an aura of leadership and direction. A rich purple carpet broadcasts a message of big ideas and creativity along with luxury. Gold decor enhances trust and loyalty. Money and balance are represented through the addition of green plants.

THE OPEN-PLAN OFFICE

The open-plan office, where many people share the same large space, presents its own problems. Human beings are territorial, and given to productivity-sapping anxiety when personal space is encroached. Some offices solve this through dividers. Color is an important factor in their effectiveness. Browns and dark greens create isolation and drain morale. Individual colors enhance the feeling of personal space, and a color appropriate to the task at hand can enhance productivity, lifting the spirit. Neutral ceilings, walls, or carpets provide the sense of common-task between the workspaces. For example, make the overall decor a basic cream, then introduce some bright colors, such as orange, emerald green, rose, and rich blue, for the paintwork. If only one color is possible, choose a bright turquoise as this creates the necessary feeling of privacy. Employees can introduce their own personal colors within their spaces.

THE FRENETIC CITY OFFICE

High pressure activities like sales and the stock market need energetic colors. Red-covered upholstery is a good place to start. Strong, hot colors create zest, energy, and drive, and literally put the workers in the hot seat! Green walls and carpets balance the red and reduce headaches that occur due to work pressure. Black, orange, and white decor will definitely give out signals of expansion and of the entrepreneur's control.

THE OFFICE AT HOME

Often the greatest challenge of working at home is stopping the work penetrating into the personal life. Royal blue carpets, yellow curtains, and pale blue or primrose-yellow walls in the office-space is a combination that should successfully keep the business where it belongs.

Wherever the office is located, and whatever function it performs, don't forget to consider the details, such as stationery. The personalized colors make a statement about the business. For example, abandon classic white paper: it can cause distraction from the written word. A careful consideration of the company's desired image plus a reference to Chapter 2, The Psychology of Color (pages 16–53), will allow you to craft an appropriate color message for your letterhead or logo.

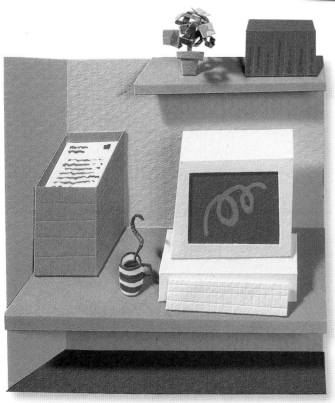

TOP LEFT

Yellow walls in a home office encourage the ideas to flow. Use a blue carpet to keep work from invading your personal life.

ABOVE

Red upholstery puts you in the hot seat and black represents unexplored opportunities. A green carpet will minimize stress.

TOP RIGHT

For an open plan office use a basic cream to give a feeling of space, but allow the workers to introduce their own personal colors.

ABOVE

Rich purple gives an impression of luxury and power. The gold wall enhances loyalty and trust.

Color in Other Environments

OTHER ENVIRONMENTS THAT we may spend time in also benefit from a well thought-out use of color.

Factories

In general, the same principles apply to the factory floor—and other workplaces—as in the home. Start by considering what the space is used for, and decide how you wish to influence the people who use it. Bright, intense colors are used in places where you want to keep people moving: in corridors, restrooms, and on assembly lines where a fast pace is required. Where people need to concentrate, muted colors are preferable, particularly those that reduce eyestrain and restlessness. Where the temperature of the workspace is high, cooler colors such as green or blue are beneficial, and where conditions are chilly, warmer tones of ivory, cream, or peach provide a lift.

Refining the application even further, where the products being assembled are themselves highly colored, the color of the immediate workspace can have a dramatic effect. A classic example comes from a lipstick factory, where the intense reds of the products were producing nausea and severe headaches among the assemblers. All of these problems disappeared when the workspace was simply painted green. Where white items are produced, blues, yellows, and greens have been found to be excellent for relieving eyestrain.

Machinery is color-coded for safety, depending on what various parts of the machine do. The areas not involved in the action of the machine—its frame, stand, and non-moving parts—should be painted a neutral color so as to not distract the operator. Attention is focused on the "working" part of the machine with colors that provide the best visibility while reducing eyestrain. Dangerous parts of the machine are highlighted in bright, warning colors such as red or yellow.

An interesting and unexpected factor in applying color in the workplace, is the discovery that colors can even affect our perception of the passage of time! In a number of experiments, light, brightly colored workspaces seem to make the day go faster!

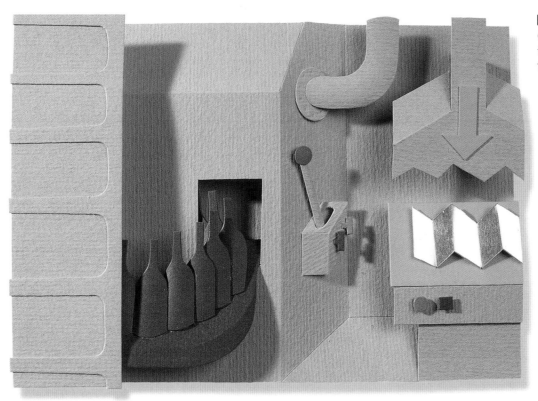

LEFT
Color-coding is vital for safety on the factory floor.

Lavender is most beneficial for the post-operative release of anesthetics.

Hospitals

In addition to the effects of color on the space and shape of rooms, hospitals dealing with emotionally disturbed people have found that the right shade of blue has a beneficial calming effect. When patient rooms are considered, it is best to use cream as a basis for the color decor, then introduce the appropriate accompanying color in drapes and accessories, according to the ailment or condition. Supplement cream with gold for depressives, turquoise for nervous complaints, red for sluggish circulation and blockages, and blue for high blood pressure. Recovery rooms would benefit from lavender, to help clear away the anesthetic.

It is also important that you think carefully about the color of the flowers that you take to a patient. Take blue and indigo for the post-operative period, when the patient needs rest. When they are ready to start moving around, introduce reds and oranges to activate the body's healing energy. Use green for nausea or biliousness.

Prisons, Schools, and Sports Grounds

Some prisons have discovered that using a mild pink for short periods reduces tension and disturbances. But, it must be very pale: too much red in it can rebound and actually cause disruptions.

A teacher who had problems with an unruly class at morning assembly advised his class, while still in the classroom, to imagine an opening in the tops of their heads, and a beautiful turquoise light flowing in. They not only loved it, they were well-behaved in the following assembly, and the teacher was summoned by the principal to explain the dramatic turnaround in their behavior! Bright yellow is another color beneficial to schools, increasing concentration at examination time.

Where the right color can calm things down, the wrong color, of course, can make things worse. It has been suggested that yellow be excluded from sports grounds and athletic events, since an overload of yellow can cause arguments and create friction.

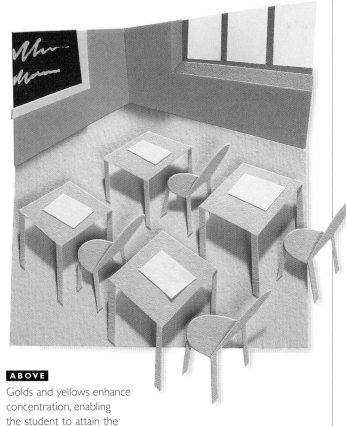

Golds and yellows enhance concentration, enabling the student to attain the best results.

Color Your Clothes

INDUSTRY AND MARKETING have long been aware of the impact that color in fashion has on the public. So too should we become conscious of the messages and signals that the clothes we wear give to others. Quite simply, the colors we wear are our calling-card. By our colors shall we be known. The colors of the clothes we choose affect not only us but the people we come into contact with. Although the body will actually absorb little of the color's vibration from the clothes, the color will, nonetheless, have a profound impact upon our psyche, which in turn creates a marked difference in our emotions and moods.

Why are we drawn to certain colors, or perhaps only one and not the others? As with food colors, we are attracted because on a certain level within us, we need that particular color's vibration to rectify an imbalance in our systems, whether it be mental, physical, or spiritual. Unfortunately, because we have become unbalanced we are inclined toward the colors that support the imbalance, rather than those that address the disturbance. It is akin to the nervous person wanting a cigarette, the depressed person needing drugs or alcohol. These patterns can be broken through the use of turquoise and blue, colors that gently calm the system. Indigo gives support for relief from addictions.

We can also use color to travel back through our lives to remember what was happening to us at any particular time. If you cannot recall events in your life when you were 15, just recall which color you favored in clothing, and this will give valuable clues as to your motivation and state of being during that period. Again, read Chapter 2, The Psychology of Color (pages 16–53), for interpretation. I wore a lot of blue in my middle teens, which indicates that, on a hindrance level, I was stuck in a rut. I certainly was! But I also had blue's patience in accepting that which could not be changed, and by examining the truth of it brought about its own healing, enabling me to become free to move on.

It is important to learn the language of color before you invest in expensive items of clothing. Fashion's trendy visual effect is the ultimate goal, completely ignoring color's vibrational qualities for health and healing, but you can think about color healing before you buy. How often have you chosen clothes the night before to wear the next morning and upon rising realized that it is the last thing you want to wear? It seemed fine then, but somehow, over night, it isn't! During sleep your body's chemistry changes, so your vibrational needs for color will be different from one day to the next. Unmet color needs can compel us to make unnecessary purchases. So, if you really *must* have that expensive flaming red sweater you've just seen, but finances are a little short, buy a red light bulb, take it home, and sit under its glow for 20 minutes. You may find that you now don't seem to have that compelling urge to purchase the garment, because you've given yourself the color's vibration which was the healing tonic, the boost your body was screaming out for. And you've also saved your money!

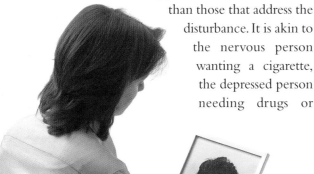

LEFT
The color of your clothing worn in the past gives a clue to how you expressed your feelings and emotions to yourself and others.

RIGHT
Expansive colors embrace the yellow of joy and laughter, enabling orange to lighten the load.

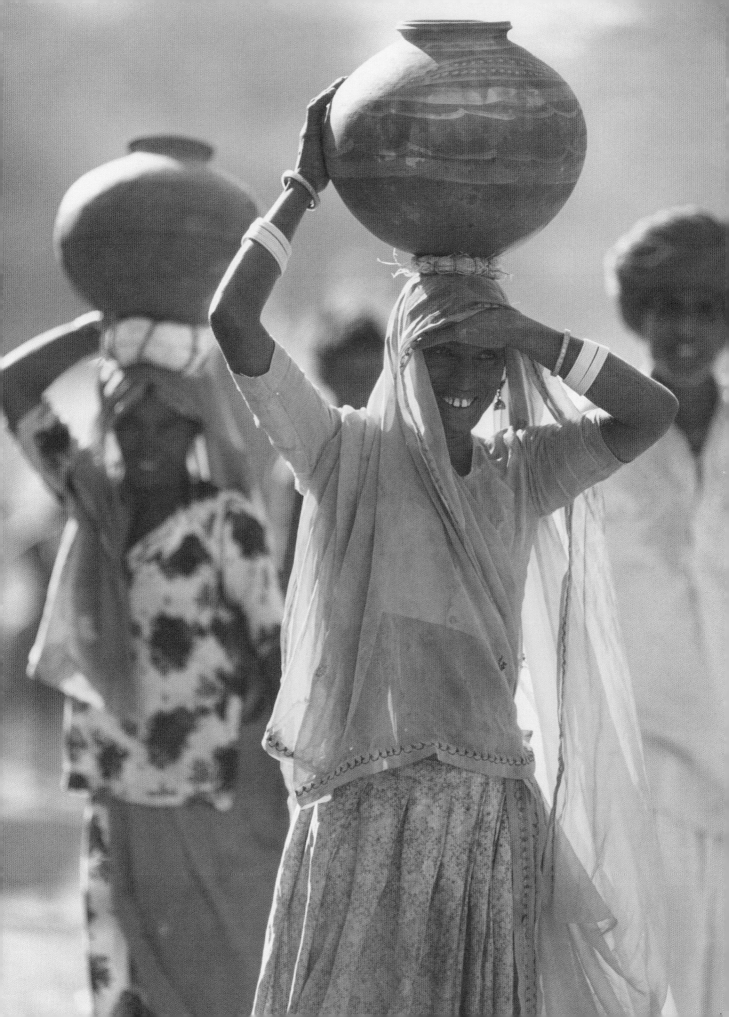

Choosing Colors for Effect

When grouping colors together, remember that the dominant hue will direct and focus your system. Use the colors for physical health and emotional benefits. Wear red for sluggish circulation, orange to combat times of fear and grief, and the blues for the release of stress. Be aware of balance, and don't overload with one color because you think it will help you feel better. Try wearing it one day at a time, and if there is no improvement after seven days, leave it for a week and try again. It you feel a color you have worn has been too much, wear something green for a day to neutralize the effect. If there is a color you realize would benefit you, but you can't stand it, wear it hidden from sight, as underwear for example—your body will still respond to its vibration.

When seeking to utilize the healing benefits of clothes, combining as many colors as possible in one outfit is not recommended. Three at the most is best for health—having first selected the colors for their specific benefits—since more than that disperses the healing qualities. For a general tonic, a medley of colors can be enjoyed for up to eight hours at a time, but not on consecutive days. Three times a week is appropriate as a treatment.

Need a loan from your bank manager? Then a somber gray will do nicely. Banks always say hooray for gray! Team it with green, the color for money. Are you

looking to make an impact with your clothes at an interview, and need to appear bright and alert? Add a little gold and yellow to show that you can be trusted, and are able to come up with interesting ideas. Do you wish to employ somebody who will be a support, contented to be in the wings and hold the fort for you? Then anyone with a hint of brown on their backs should be hired immediately. Nervous of speaking in front of a crowd? Then allow the turquoise vibration in an item of clothing to steady and calm you.

Colors worn at a certain age are also indicative. Pink and black are good examples. Pink worn by a young girl shows she is ready to develop her full potential. In a mature woman of 50 plus, it indicates reassessment time, and a possible need to melt old ideas and issues. Teenagers in black leather are making the statement that

RIGHT
The cerise jacket displays her womanhood, with her full mauve skirt signifying that she is a woman of distinction and dignity.

LEFT
His tan shirt shows a quiet assurance, with black's power of judgment.

FAR LEFT
The sombre grays give the impression of stability and steadfastness. Note the colors added to gray to pinpoint their intentions, representing go-ahead and initiative.

they are ready to take control of their own lives and run the world. They believe they can do a better job of making the universe work than their predecessors did. They are no longer willing to let their parents, or society, tell them what to do. Black worn obsessively by people in their 20s or 30s indicates that something has brought the person's life to a halt. Their life is on hold and they feel boxed in. By the age of 40, how we relate to black shows how we have come to terms with power and control. Generally, when assessing anyone wearing black, see if there is another color with it, since this will show physiologically what the person's expectations are.

There are unlimited combinations of colored clothes that you can use to enhance your life. Regard colored clothes as ingredients and be selective. Use color to aid and abet you in your daily endeavors. If the boss is wearing a black suit with a pink shirt or tie, tread carefully because someone is about to get fired!

4 Relationships and Children

Color plays a significant part in your loving relationships and your children's well-being. This section helps you to choose the right color for your child and teaches you how to connect with people. Love is the transformer; it helps you to learn. To communicate in a loving relationship, you must take courage in one hand and doubt in the other—they are partners. The biggest misconception we make about love is that someone will give it to us, when, in fact, relationships are a skill we learn.

RELATIONSHIPS HAVE THEIR crises, their ups and downs, and usually we blame the other person for making us feel this way. Just remember, you are both in love in order to learn what love is. Falling in love is never done sensibly, but we use it as the basis for a lifetime's commitment—marriage. People fall in love because of their matching jigsaw patterns dovetailing neatly into each other: the good pieces as well as the fears, insecurities, and vulnerabilities.

Ultimately, relationships are based on emotions. You cannot have fulfillment in relationships unless you understand the fundamental beliefs, pictures, or ideals that you have taken on as a man or woman. All activities

Color can reveal the significance of that which underlies or undermines our relationships.

HEALING COLOR/EMOTION CHART

Primary emotions and their causes with related colors for healing.

EMOTION	COLOR	SITUATION	HEALING COLOR
Grief/sorrow	Brown	Loss of loved one	ORANGE
Fear	Black	Threat	PINK
Anger	Red	Obstacle	BLUE
Joy	Yellow	Potential mate	GREEN
Trust	Gold	Group member	ORANGE
Disgust	Mustard	Gruesome object	INDIGO
Anticipation	Orange	New territory	RED
Surprise	Yellow	Sudden novel object	GOLD
Desolation	Gray	Made to feel unwanted	PURPLE
Jealousy	Dark green	Made to feel insecure	RED
Guilt	Dark red	Made to feel not good enough	YELLOW

FIVE BASIC RELATIONSHIP COLOR PATTERNS

1. THE MARTYR

RELATES TO THE NEGATIVE		CORRECTIVE HEALING COLOR
DARK BLUE	Never stops worrying. They intend to make you pay for their martyrdom. They suffer in silence, but still manage to wear it like a badge.	PINK

2. THE PERFECTIONIST

RELATES TO THE NEGATIVE		CORRECTIVE HEALING COLOR
DARK PURPLE	Into control. When they were young they were never told they did well, even when they did. So now nothing their partner does will be quite good enough either. Results in the bully.	YELLOW

3. THE BUTTERFLY

RELATES TO THE NEGATIVE		CORRECTIVE HEALING COLOR
DARK ORANGE	Flits here and there. Never going into anything very deeply. Always skimming through relationships. Avoids getting into anything that might be heavy. Fear of failure—so why bother. A classic remark is "Don't be silly, dear."	INDIGO

4. THE CARETAKER

RELATES TO THE NEGATIVE		CORRECTIVE HEALING COLOR
DARK GREEN	"I can only get my needs met if I'm seen to be doing it, looking after everyone." Continually cleaning, vacuuming. Great rage here: flicking the duster—beating the carpet with a stick. In the male it's the home improvement freak.	RED

5. WORKAHOLIC

RELATES TO THE NEGATIVE		CORRECTIVE HEALING COLOR
DARK RED	Relationships come last on their list. Everything else comes first. No trust that there is anything else. It's the career woman in the family, or the workaholic male.	BLUE

have a pattern, and color can reveal those patterns. Every feeling and emotion has a color of its own. Use the chart to help start the healing process. Various methods are given throughout the book for incorporating healing color into the system.

An emotion is a chemical event that is experienced in the body. Every time you communicate with a partner or loved one, an emotion happens first. If you feel uncomfortable with any of the emotions encountered between you and your mate, use the appropriate healing color given to counteract the negative emotions.

Relationship Patterns

Relationships fall into patterns. Counselors see the same relationship patterns time after time. In the relationships color patterns chart above are listed five common patterns and their color connections. Do you recognize any of them? Do you fit into any of these roles? Or have you ever had a relationship with any of these people? Which one are you?

To incorporate the corrective color, eat, drink, or wear the color, use it in decor, or treat yourself to a bowl of colored fruit or flowers.

RIGHT
Color can bring a higher degree of unity and intimacy to your relationship.

Compatibility

The best time to make your relationship well is before it becomes sick. All relationships have periods of stress and discord which bring on periods of reactive fighting and distancing. Distancing and fighting are not the problem between any two people—they are normal ways of managing anxiety. The level of anxiety in any relationship, however, depends on how much has been brought in by the two partners from sources both past and present. This has a direct reflection in compatibility.

Compatibility is the ability to exist together harmoniously. As any couple will probably confirm, it is easier to define than achieve. The fact is that no matter how much two people care for each other, they are going to have areas where their personalities come into conflict.

It is a natural instinct to have relationships. Without relationships the species dies. We are drawn to relationships continuously because relationships are all that we have in life. We all work with positive and negative patterns with our partner—it's called growth. But we often fall into arguments of "I'm right, he's wrong" and vice versa, both arguing to win instead of arguing to progress. One partner may criticize, but usually it's not constructive criticism—it doesn't tell you how to change. It is black and white thinking.

Feelings of love can easily be spoken and often they are. But "I love you" can also be used as a defense, to make the other person happy in the hope that they'll back off and not get too close. It's not what you say, but how you show it.

Find a partner who supports you, and lets you support yourself. Choose a partner who wants you to win. A partner who wants you to get what you want just as much as you do. Remember, they will be doing the same.

COLOR COMPATIBILITY PROCESS

Would you like to know the current state of your relationship? Is there something that you haven't been able to resolve by talking? The Color Compatibility Process can give you information that you might not have been able to uncover. It helps us to see clearly how we operate with partners, a discovery that makes our lives much easier. We can learn to free ourselves from unfulfilling patterns and resolve any dissatisfaction. You cannot have fulfillment in relationships unless you understand what is going on. Discovering each other's color-energy blocks stops either of you becoming stuck in a rut.

There are many understandings to each hue. To decide which aspect applies, use what I call "perceptive psychology," commonly known as intuition. Reveal to each other the color chosen so that you can share and resolve your differences by the use of color language. The process enables you to examine the love problem that you have with each other. You may work with this process alone to gain an insight into a relationship if you wish. Use the process to gain a new lease-of-love with your partner.

THE COLOR COMPATIBILITY PROCESS

1. To begin the process, start bonding by holding hands for three minutes, and visualize a golden-colored wind blowing between you. Release hands.

2. At a table, sit side by side or facing each other. Sit together but not touching. Place your hands shoulder-width apart in front of you, on the table, with your palms facing inward, ready to encapture the color of your relationship. Close your eyes and breathe in deeply and slowly. Breathe out slowly. Do this three times, or until you both feel relaxed and comfortable.

3. With your eyes still closed, imagine that you are placing your love for your partner onto the table before you, which will appear between your hands as a misty, colored ball. If you cannot see a color, simply choose one, it will be just as effective.

4. Look at the color for a minute or two in your mind's eye. Notice whether the color changes, or if more than one color enters. After five minutes, set a timer if you wish, take a deep breath in. Release the colored ball, and open your eyes.

5. Sit quietly for a while, focusing your attention on the color, or colors, that you saw in your ball.

6. The next stage is to examine the meaning of the colors you have just visualized using The Color Declarations discussed over the next few pages. Pinpoint which aspects of the colors, shades, or tints that you saw relate to you and your partner. If you didn't visualize any of the spectrum colors which follow, then refer to Chapter 2, The Psychology of Color, and read the "shade" or "tint" sections to receive your understandings. The color you have chosen relates to how you feel about your partner. From the color declaration, you will be able to use your intuition to achieve key insights into your relationship.

7. The language of color has just spoken to you, and now it is time to take a risk and discuss the appropriate color selection with your partner. You will be enlightening him or her as to how you feel about the relationship right now. Here is an opportunity to use a new language—the language of color—to bring new and meaningful communication into your relationship.

BELOW
Let the language of color
speak to you through the
Color Compatibility Process.

The Color Declarations

RED DECLARATION

Experiencing red in the Color Compatibility Process can indicate that the physical side of a relationship has its difficulties. Reds and pinks convey our feelings about intimacy, and particularly that aspect of it known as "the sex drive." Touching, caressing, kissing, every phase and variety of physical intimacy are in the domain of red. Red can show that one partner feels there is a problem with physical contact. It may be that one partner is more highly sexed than the other, causing rejection pain when the loved one does not respond. The balance of red is to aim for passion without pain.

The red in your process can also show that you are bored. Boredom in a relationship is caused by energy locked up inside. It is rage, deeply repressed anger. Boredom creates a loss of communication in relationships. You don't want to face up to what really is. In clamping down against the anger you become bored. Beat a few pillows to release the rage. Seek a sex therapist's advice if necessary. If sexual intimacy is suppressed, depression occurs. Red can also indicate that bullying may be present because of one partner's need to dominate.

REPAIRING ACTION: Start kissing and cuddling just for the sake of it.

ORANGE DECLARATION

Visualizing orange in the Color Compatibility Process highlights sociability and the interaction of the couple with other people. Have you ever been out with someone at a gathering only to find that your partner has vanished into the crowd? You get the distinct feeling they are more worried about their impression upon others than they are about you? The partner receiving an "orange" imbalanced love can feel distinctly dumped. Are you doing this or is it happening to you? Does either one of you show off at parties, or always insist on paying for the drinks? The boastfulness may be just a protection to prove to themselves that they are really liked and desirable. The secret fear, resulting from a feeling of inferiority, is that the other partner might leave them. If breakups have been experienced in the relationship already, then the partner has not got over it yet. If you can't stand your partner flirting you have two choices, stay and ignore it or move on. Orange may also indicate thoughts of divorce.

REPAIRING ACTION: Cut out any practical jokes. They're not funny; they're unkind.

YELLOW DECLARATION

Yellow is usually seen in the Color Compatibility Process when nagging, complaining, and criticism come into a relationship. Nagging is a sign of unhappiness, which can affect the nerves. The joy has gone, and happiness is destroyed. Usually there is an expectation of love that is unrealistic. Thoughts are scattered. You both talk and talk and yet get nowhere. Total bickering and arguing eventually leads to isolation and non-communication. You may also believe that you will never be good enough and that your partner is much cleverer than you are. The underlying belief is actually the reverse: "If I was in a relationship with someone else, I know it would be better." In this case there is a lack of confidence within that person. What they are searching for is safety within a relationship. Being too scared to take a risk in life results in a shallow partnership, skimming over the surface, and without depth. The relationship is on a fickle footing, and there is an inclination to use the marriage as a social ladder, a feeling of "I married beneath me."

REPAIRING ACTION: Start laughing together again in order to release the tension, and seek a solid direction for the relationship. Go on vacation together and try to loosen up.

GREEN DECLARATION

Green loving has two sides to it, being a compound of blue and yellow. It has what has been called "the worm-that-turned syndrome," coming from the blue side. The relationship has reached a point where the old ways of thinking and being will no longer do.

The yellow side of green, the "turn," usually occurs at mid-life crisis, which is anything from 35 years up to 60. Green at this period can change from seeming contentment to "Just a minute! This is my space and no one is going to stop me taking it. Move over!" The partner wants to experience their rightful place and not be put upon, and relinquish doing things at the expense of themselves. It explains why individuals leave a relationship after 30 years, leaving the other partner completely stunned.

When green follows its heart, nothing is unobtainable. Above all, green wants to bring harmony to the home and to affairs of the heart. Unfortunately, jealousy's possessiveness, money problems, and "smother-love" can also rear their ugly heads with troubled green. Declaration greens can become more sensual with possessions than with people.

REPAIRING ACTION: Share an intimate dinner with exotic, luscious fruits.

BLUE DECLARATION

A blue visualization truly can be recognized as loneliness and isolation—the big chasm in any relationship. A typical blue scene is in a restaurant, the couple sitting opposite each other, both with glazed eyes, staring into space. Not a spark is going on between them, literally nothing being said. The partnership is stuck in a rut. A lethargy has developed. There seems to be a feeling that there is nothing that they can do about it. Helpless and hopeless. This feeling often results when the partner's mother was anesthetized in labor, and the infant's feeling of paralysis is the subconscious belief later brought into relationships. Active rebirthing therapy processes can relieve this. You need to realize that you don't have to accept this, that you're not a helpless victim of circumstances any more.

Blue also depicts an emotional coldness, a painful experience for the recipient. Or perhaps there is emotional manipulation going on—which can be very tiring to cope with. To release yourself from martyrdom can only be an improvement all-round, particularly for the partner, because martyrs are such a strain to live with. If you are hooked into serving a martyr, heed this motto to all do-gooders "I have drunk your tears and they have poisoned me."

REPAIRING ACTION: Get active together—join a gym or take some form of regular exercise.

INDIGO DECLARATION

When indigo is seen on the table before you, it shows restriction in a relationship, the pattern where one partner cannot let go of control, and allow the other to hold the fort for a while. This derives from the black in the blue which makes indigo. Indigo indicates a rigidity of rules, both spoken and unspoken. Usually the rules have not been questioned. Are they relevant to us as a couple? Do we need to follow them? Although indigo has a devotional quality, it can be very limiting. When indigo appears, the whole structure and nature of the relationship needs reassessing and reviewing. Watch for selfishness and addictive patterns—always doing the same routines. The backbone of the relationship is not straight!

Indigo can also indicate a relationship held together out of gratitude. A debt of gratitude is the most humiliating debt of all. Such are the insidious roots of gratitude, they suck you dry. Release from gratitude is, in a way, organic. Indigo is rather inclined to the drama of life, so one or both partners may tussle for center stage.

REPAIRING ACTION: Book some theater tickets or join an amateur dramatic group as an outlet. It is time to get real.

DUAL COLORS

You may see a second color in your process. Just look to both their meanings and see which aspect applies to you. Use also the "shade" and "tint" interpretation of the colors featured in Chapter 2, The Psychology of Color. Again, let color resolve your differences and let your instincts guide you to the specific interpretation related to your relationship. Accept your colors. Trust the truth, your inner self. It doesn't cheat you. Neither does color.

PURPLE DECLARATION

Because "purple loving" has red and blue in it, it has two points of view. Either the partner has a desire to be totally in charge of the arrangements and the leader of the couple, laying down all the rules—relating to the red—or they are totally disconnected and don't wish to come down to earth at all, remaining a child—relating to the blue. They prefer to be up in the clouds, which means they are not much use to themselves, or anyone else for that matter. Manipulation can be a force here also, coming from the blue aspect. There is nothing more deadly than the emotionally immature child-partner.

If the partner is coming from the red aspect of the purple, they are so critical of themselves, the perfectionist, that it's hard for anyone to come up to their standards. Purple can also be rather in love with love, or with their own social standing. Although they may take a leading role in the community as well as within the relationship, they are usually isolated and unapproachable, making life very difficult for their mate. They need to visualize themselves playing an instrument in the orchestra instead of being the maestro. The aspects missing from the relationship are comradeship and friendship. A little more humor would also help.

REPAIRING ACTION: Swap roles for a week to allow humility and appreciation to enter the relationship.

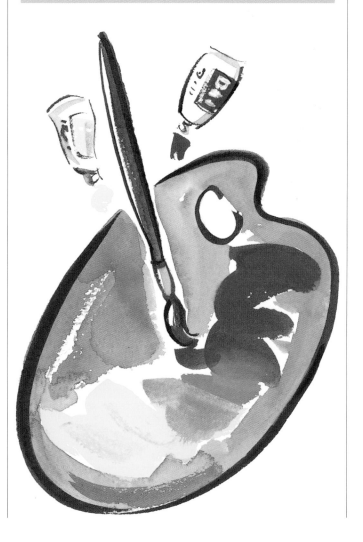

The Turquoise Unity Process

After completing the Color Compatibility Process with your partner, now use the Turquoise Unity Process to begin closing the gap that separates your hearts' desires. This process will prepare you to move into the next stage of your relationship.

Green, blue, and yellow together produce turquoise. Turquoise causes a unity and progression in any relationship, the realization that the only way out of a stressful situation is through the yellow of communication. When the green of the heart and blue of the throat join together some pretty plain yellow speaking—perhaps arguing—can result, but with all three colors combined in turquoise as the healer, it can be fantastic making up afterward!

To carry out the healing process:
1. Sit facing each other, and join hands. Visualize yourselves surrounded by a rich turquoise mist that you both draw into yourselves through the top of your head.
2. See your entire body filling with turquoise. Then, through your joined hands, send brilliant turquoise light to each other, filling your partner with its radiance.
3. Just sit silently for a minute or two. The inner you, and that of your partner, will complete the moment in a way appropriate to the needs of your relationship.

RELATIONSHIPS

Coming together is a beginning.

Keeping together is progress.

Working together is success.

Unconditional Love—In the Pink

Books and personal growth training teach the importance of loving oneself. The first stage of any successful relationship is that which we have with ourselves. Love is the only effective cure there is. Unfortunately, it isn't that easy. I have witnessed participants literally walking

LOVING YOURSELF

1. Breathe pink breath. With your eyes closed, visualize a soft pink haze surrounding you and inhale the color for one minute.

2. Allow your left hand to become a soft fist, holding it and cradling it with your right hand for one minute.

3. Still keeping the left hand a fist, gently stroke the top part of the back of the hand with the index and middle fingers of the right hand.

4. Encircle the fist again with the right hand and very, very slowly lift the fist up to your lips so that they caress and kiss the back of the hand.

5. Bring the fist to the chest on the heart center, and hold it there while taking a deep, pink breath, filling your body full of love, and exhaling out all doubt and despair.

around with clenched fists muttering to themselves "I will love myself"—even if it kills them. A simple process can enable you to connect to that all-giving, loving self that you possess.

Give yourself a kiss. Use the color pink, it has an emotional understanding of the consistency of love, affection, and contentment, all the attributes that are harnessed when we connect to our loving self. You have just given yourself unconditional love. You do not have to wait ever again for someone else to give love and affection to you. Repeat the process as often as you wish—there is plenty more for you where that came from.

RIGHT
The Turquoise Unity Process brings a new level of intimacy and harmony to your relationship.

Color Care for Children

CHILDREN ARE NATURAL healers. You do not have to diagnose them in depth and then rack your brains for a cure. If you have a sick child in bed you just show them a range of colors and ask them to choose the one they like best. They always pick the color they need for healing. They are "naturals" intuitively. They automatically go for what is right for them. As adults we need to learn to synchronize the color with the right ailment or condition by consciously tuning in. Anyone who listens is a healer: it is not only the laying-on of hands. Listen to your child and he will instinctively tell you what his needs are through the aid of color.

To do this simple test with your child, just collect together every color you can; they can be in the form of crayons, papers, a set of cards, pieces of material, or maybe a selection of paint cards from decorating stores. Put the colors together in a box so that the child can select one. Just ask the child which one they like the best, and then introduce that color into their system through food, clothing, lighting, and so on.

The psychological effect that color has on children is very powerful. The colors discussed in this section are specifically for children. When choosing a color for your child from the Color Acupressure Directions (see pages 108–113), or from Chapter 2, The Psychology of Color, remember to use it sparingly, since children usually need less than half the adult exposure.

General Health

An easy and pleasant way to treat a sick child is to flood their room with the appropriate color. It is painless, in fact. You have nothing to lose by inserting a blue light bulb in the lamp overnight if the child has a fever, since blue is good for healing infections and fretfulness, and soothes and reduces high temperatures. This simple "illumination" is recommended for children who are sick or have behavioral problems. Another effective way to flood them with color healing is in the decor of their bedroom—which doesn't mean that every time a child has a cold you have to change the color of his room. Simply change the color of the bedclothes, rugs, or drapes to introduce the necessary healing power. The appropriate color must be carefully chosen for all conditions and the time of exposure monitored if using chromotherapy.

It is extremely depressing to put children into dull beige or brown bedrooms. Brown is a repressive color for children under the age of ten. A sensitive child constantly surrounded with browns and dark beiges will become lethargic, withdrawn, and depressive, inclined to sit in a heap, static and dull. Brown is fine in a living area for adults and children together, but not for a bedroom for a young child. Young children like soft colors such as peach, blue, spring yellow, warm cream, and pink. If the child likes blue, balance the bedroom by adding peach pinks and creams. If they prefer warm colors introduce lavender, blue, and lilac as well. Yellow will help a child concentrate, but should only be used in a very pale shade for the under eights. When it comes to exam time in the teenage years the color can be made stronger, to help with concentration.

LEFT
If your child has a fever, use a blue lightbulb in their lamp for a soothing and calming effect.

RIGHT
Soft colors such as warm cream and blue are ideal for children's bedrooms

ABOVE
Connection to pink allows unconditional love to enter, fulfilling deep desires and wishes.

Conception, Fertility, and Infertility: Pink and Yellow, Orange and Red

A mother should prepare herself for pregnancy. It is akin to preparing the soil before the seed is planted. Sometimes, a woman subconsciously feels she is not good enough to be pregnant. This is where the pink comes in. Pink is connected to the female reproductive system. A lack of deep rose pink can affect one into feeling unlovable, unwomanly, childless. Wear this color, eat it, have it on your walls, and your bedsheets. It will bring about your desires. I advised one woman to use this pink combined with yellow and within the year she was pregnant. Yellow enables you to receive the wisdom that you are a lovely, loveable person and is also good for the nervous system. Yellow helps one to achieve. A small amount of mauve is also useful as an aid toward conception.

For the male, the colors for infertility are orange and red, applied accordingly—they are also useful for impotence. Red aids virility. Blue is the color to calm the nerves of the expectant father who is anxious about the imminent birth.

When the female is pregnant she is drawn to blue. It expels fears. It is said that when we are a fetus we can see blue in the womb.

Newborn and Infants: White

It is very interesting to note that a mother's milk is a transparent silvery white, linked to the ethereal cord to which the baby was connected a short while ago, the attachment to the spiritual world. The color white is the only color that contains every color. Even from birth, Mother Nature is giving us, by mouth, our survival food: every color that we need, in minute, balanced quantities. Even when we are too undeveloped to choose the perfect colored food for ourselves, our mother has it neatly ready for us. That is why it is not good to wean a baby too soon—four to six months at the earliest.

It is customary practice to dress babies in white because it is mistakenly considered a "non-color." In fact it is quite right to use white, but only because it is full of every color. It is also advisable to use other pale, soft colors in the decor surrounding a baby, such as pinks, blues, peach, eau-de-Nil, but not stark white, as you do not wish to overload. Use white for the paintwork, but use a pastel shade for the walls and definitely do not use reds—not if you want your baby to get any rest! The trauma of birth is quite enough without being stimulated and shocked by a strongly colored nursery.

In the United States, tests showed that putting babies who were jaundiced at birth into blue baths had a profound effect in curing them. At least 30,000 babies have received this therapy, illustrating the healing power of color even on the newborn.

ABOVE
Wrapping babies in white surrounds them with all-giving openness and unity.

RIGHT
The white rose is the host to every color, and favors none. It is the symbol of peace.

LEFT
Pink for a girl is yin; blue for boys is yang—it is the eternal polarity.

Birth to 18 Months: Pink and Blue

It is very important to remember that what you wear on the outside travels through to the inside. Pink is the feminine child color for the newborn up to 18 months. The clear, soft pink represents a child's love and protects against childhood fears. If a boy child cries, put him in pink and it will balance him. Soft blue is the boy child color, but if a boy baby is aggressive, wrap him in something pink. If your baby girl has her needs met and still cries, put something blue on her for balance. Pink is yin, blue is yang—male and female. Pink helps the child to learn to give and receive love, and to love itself and the human race. It is vital with infants to keep the balance of pink and blue in both sexes.

Blue is very good for teething troubles. It is a cooler, and it also aids sleep. Don't forget blue for the treatment of fever and sickness as well.

Toddlers from Two to Four Years: Pale Green

After eighteen months—the enquiring time when children start to become mobile and are beginning to learn about the world around them—your child can be put into soft apple green. This is the time when everything has to be put out of reach, when nothing is safe from inquisitive hands and minds. This period is extremely important, as their decision-making is developing. This is the crucial time for the development of self-confidence. If the child is not allowed to explore and experience all around him, when he reaches his teenage years he will not be able to decide what he wants to be or do. At this early stage in life, like new shoots and buds, children start to move and grow, so let them taste dirt and feel its texture. They are learning to experience their own judgment. Pale green is the stabilizer. Pale lemon will also help develop intelligence. Yellow is the wisdom the child is searching for. Give your toddler a yellow cuddly toy—it will make for joy and happiness.

When your child starts learning to talk, give him or her lots of blue. Blue is connected to the throat chakra (see pages 98–99), so concentrate the color in this area. It will promote and develop speech. Blue is also the great

cooler for tender skin and minor rashes. If your child is unfortunate enough to get sunstroke, heal the redness and irritation using pale to bluebell blue, not the dark shade. However, if a child is in severe pain, use a strong blue or indigo for a short period.

When a little older, about four or five, if a child is too sensitive and pale looking, apply soft green with pink. This will boost the confidence. If, at this age, the child displays aggressive behavior—the child who bites their friends—apply soft green as well. This will help to counteract their frustration. Enjoy this short green stage, when your child looks to you for everything—a sweet springtime which all too soon passes.

ABOVE
Pale yellow will help to develop your toddler's intelligence; pale green will stabilize temperament.

RIGHT
A kaleidoscope of color will help develop your child's full potential.

Starting School: Orange

Orange helps a schoolchild to achieve. When a child comes up to school age, introduce a little pale peach for confidence. This is the time when "teacher knows best," and the child parrots everything the teacher says as he or she begins confidently to explore the outside world. Peach is lovely for the timid and fearful child as it will give security and interest in his work. If a child is indifferent to color, give or apply peach if young, or orange if older, about 12 years, as these colors give the child the chance to expand their abilities and horizons. Orange also gives strength and courage. Do not use too much orange in decor and clothes, however, but use it to boost the child for a short period only.

Peach has white in it and is a dilution of orange. To overload young children with strong orange makes them mature, emotionally and mentally, before their time. They will miss out on their childhood, leading to problems later on, particularly in their 40s or during the mid-life crisis. It can strain a child, but the power of orange in therapy to stimulate children with learning difficulties has been used to great effect. It helps to expand their vision on life. Orange curtains or cushions have been incorporated to stimulate backward children. Orange clothing can be worn according to the degree of under-development.

There is much research being carried out into the use of glasses with colored lenses to help the dyslexic child. There are many forms of dyslexia and different colors can help, particularly with reading difficulties.

Soft, pale, clear pink is good for the bed-wetter. Bed-wetting occurs when the child feels unlovable. It is known that boys have this problem more than girls. He doesn't love himself for a while so he wets. Let him or her start again with pink as a new beginning. It will help him to love himself once more. Unfortunately, even at birth boys are pressured into not needing anything, stunting our sons before they have a chance to be little boys.

Hyperactive children, when over-excited, respond well to clear soft green, blue, or violet. Green and violet are good colors for a child in pain or for headaches. If they are confined to bed you could use these colors as bedcovers or nightwear. Decorate their bedrooms in

ABOVE
Choose an appropriately colored bedspread for the phase of life your child is going through.

RIGHT
The peach color will comfort any child who is in distress or experiencing difficulties within the family.

these colors. For an epileptic child use leaf or grass green with pale soft pink and blue. If the attacks are severe use strong rich green. Encourage color breathing techniques, which are good for this complaint (see pages 102–103).

Many illnesses and pains come from psychological causes. Use sun-gold colors to help relieve the mental stress and fears that cause these in the child. Violet can be used as the great protector—but not purple. Violet bedroom decor or surrounds, or even clothes, will help keep him or her safe.

If stammering is a problem, use yellow for wisdom and blue for the throat. For the child who has difficulty making friends, strong pink or cerise will draw friendships. People always talk to anyone who is in the pink! Try it yourself, it works.

Broken Homes: Orange and Indigo

When children's parents divorce between the ages of four and eight, it is a great shock to them. Broken homes represent a break in everything that they do. However hard the parents may try to ease the situation, the child will go into a certain amount of shock and it is this bereavement that seems to be neglected in treatment. The child is in grief that the parents are not together. It is well proven that all children, even when they get into their teens, have the one fantasy that mom and dad will get back together again. To treat the shock—apart from counseling, which is extremely important—use the color orange. Orange will put their lives together again, and give them strength to cope with the situation.

When a child is very young it is very difficult to explain to them the reasons why their parents are apart. Under four years of age they know something is wrong, but they don't understand what is happening. For this age group, use a shade of orange, say peach or tangerine. Decorate their bedroom in it. Encourage them to eat oranges and carrots or wear the color. Use this therapy for the first year of the break-up. Apply pink for grief and also to make the child feel lovable again. The over-eights can have the situation explained to them, but they also require the added color of indigo to help them restructure themselves and their surroundings.

Teenagers: Yellow

When the teenager is half adult/half child, he struggles to learn to balance the mind and body. This is the selfish time of life, the "me, I want" time. This is the difficult period of learning to be aware of other people's needs, to give and take, not only with mother and father but with the world. No wonder it's so confusing. A little turquoise will help push the teenager off the fence into adulthood. Yellow in the turquoise will help the child who finds it difficult to concentrate. A child needs a lot of confidence at this time. It is also a time to start making a stand. If they cannot make decisions or make up their mind about anything, their second development in life, to "go for it," cannot progress. This teenager was probably repressed at the three- to five-year-old period. Hence the agonies of being a teenager, feeling unsure and inadequate. Bright blue will give confidence and soothe. It will calm them, help them to see their way clearly, give them a "reason for." Add also daffodil yellow, this will strengthen the nerves and give a little joy. However, do not over-saturate a teenager with too strong a yellow because it could stimulate a keen interest in drugs. Yellow is wisdom but you do not want the interest to be pushed to finding out about non-useful spheres. Indigo is good for counteracting drug abuse. Indigo is also the color of the skeleton of the body. When you think how drugs affect the very structure of the being, you can see how it relates.

Mid-teens is still exam time and can be very stressful. Yellow is great for studying and for the hectic period of intense pressure leading up to exams. It aids concentration. The yellow lifts and is also good for the nervous system, and combined with blue, it will soothe jangled nerves. Constipation is sometimes a problem at this stage because of so much sitting, so use yellow in clothes, surroundings, or food. Clear violet is a good protection for teenagers. It will steer and guide them on their way.

Anorexia and bulimia often develop at this time: use rich orange and deep gold for the first and yellow and violet for the latter.

BELOW
The teenage years are a sunshine time where yellow's brightness will bring in joy, laughter, and added freedom.

LEFT
Purple is related to
the new phase of
life when the last
child has left home,
but introduce
turquoise to
help you with
the transition.

For Parents—The Empty Nest: Purple

The turquoise age is when your children leave home and get married. As a parent you may feel left out now, since they have their own lives and are busy living them. You feel outdated, your ideas are old-fashioned and you are made to feel that you don't know anything. When parents favor only pale pinks and blues it indicates that they won't let go of their children. Let go. Stop tying the child down with emotions. The emotional part of the parent wants to hang on. Pink is a young child's love, but in the parent it can be a sign of clinging, smothering love.

The offspring have left the nest, they have made their own way, are gone, and they have forgotten to say "thank you." Even when you baby-sit your grand-children you are left strict instructions in case you get it wrong! Although purple, the transition color, is related to this phase in your life, turquoise is the color to introduce to encourage you to stand still and take stock. It helps you come to know yourself and what you need and want, not only for your married offspring but for yourself as a grandparent. After all, aren't you finding your own way now into a new phase of life the purple period of powerful self-assuredness?

5 Color Healing and its Techniques

While color healing has come to many people's attention only in the last two decades, it actually has a long history. In the early part of the 20th century, physician Dr. Dinshah P. Ghadiale did much to promote color medically, by healing with different colored lights. He called this process spectro-chrome-metry, called chromotherapy today. Color healing received the ultimate accolade in 1903 when the Danish physician Neils Finsen was awarded the Nobel prize for Medicine for his work on light and color in healing disease. He reported cures for over 20,000 patients using both sunlight and artificial ultraviolet light.

AS WE DISCOVER in this chapter, disease is not just a malfunction of the physical body, which is often treated as nothing more than an organic machine. The human organism is made of many interweaving and interlinked facets, some of which are physical, others purely energetic. When we are ill, we are often missing the connection to the essential part of ourselves that exists as an integral part of the natural environment. A person not fully at one with that nature becomes ill as a consequence, either physically or mentally, experiencing an ongoing sense of unease with one's self and a continuing sense of lacking something in life. Color is a powerful tool both to expose the disharmonious aspect, and to help put it right.

There are many ways of harnessing the power of color for health and well-being. Color can be eaten, worn, drunk, absorbed through your skin or eyes, or visualized. Alternatively, home and workplace can be decorated and lit specifically with color healing in mind. When using the following techniques, always refer back to Chapter 2 for guidance on the correct colors to use.

Other Color Healing Techniques and Tools

Aside from the tools and techniques described in detail in this chapter, various other pieces of equipment can be used to promote color healing. A torch or flashlight, such as the color Reflexology Crystal Torch (see Useful Addresses on page 142), can beam the appropriate color onto a pressure point while it is being stimulated. Coloring a jacuzzi bath with underwater or overhead lighting is a wonderful—and relaxing—way of combining water with color vibration. Bottles with colored liquids, such as those produced by Aura Soma (see Useful Addresses on page 142), are manufactured by several companies and can be useful in readings and treatments.

Colored salt-rubs have been successfully used to help invigorate paralyzed limbs. A white linen bag is filled with sea salt, and impregnated with color from a spotlight. The bag can then be used to gently massage the area of paralysis. The bag can also be used over the entire body for other complaints. Wrapping colored silks around the body is another wonderful way of enveloping oneself in pure color vibration. It was discovered several centuries ago that wrapping the afflicted area in red silk minimized the scarring from smallpox—an indicator of how effective the technique is. Even nothing more than a small, green silk square placed at the back of the head when sitting relieves tension and pressure.

RIGHT
Colored light is a powerful and potent tool of healing.

Energy Healing

IN RECENT YEARS, the Western world has come to accept the idea that the human body is more than just flesh and bone; that it also has components that are energetic in nature, energies that are the manifestation of universal energies. Healing therapies such as acupuncture, acupressure, reiki, and the laying on of hands, are all built on the premise that the body's energy flows can be influenced in a positive way through outside intervention. Which is, in turn, based on the belief that the body's energetic nature is both reflected in and influences the functioning of the physical body.

As we have discovered in the previous pages, the energies of color are part of the environment in which the human body evolved. Not only that, but it is only within the narrow confines of the visible spectrum that we can even survive. Therefore, it is hardly surprising that our physical bodies have a very direct relationship to color. Discovering the nature of that relationship, and how color can be used to keep the body in a state of harmony and balance—health—has been the work of color therapists and researchers for centuries.

So what is energy? The answer is, we don't know. Neither does science. We can measure its properties as heat, light, atomic forces, but nowhere can we say exactly what it is. Likewise, as we work with energy healing, we

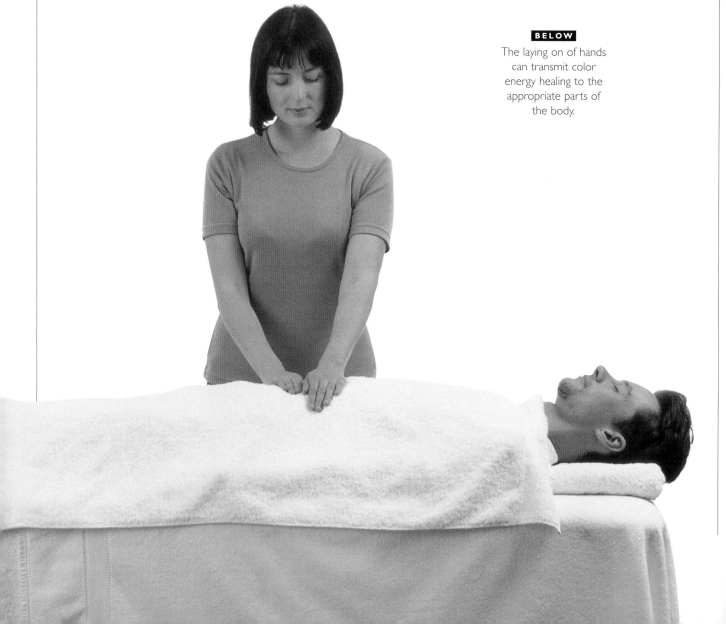

BELOW
The laying on of hands can transmit color energy healing to the appropriate parts of the body.

can observe its effects, without defining what it is. How we see its effects depends to some degree on what we are looking for. The acupuncturist looks for the lines of energy flow within the body—the meridians—that have been defined through hundreds of years of practice, and each of which has its own unique color. Acupuncturists know that the placement of needles at certain positions within that flow have an observable influence on the physical body. Acupressure does the same, but with the use of pressure rather than needles at critical points. Other therapies that use massage techniques are working on essentially the same principles.

Another way of understanding the body's energy flows is to see and study its aura. Different healers see slightly different things, but the aura is essentially the body's field of energy that extends beyond the physical. It is usually seen as a number of colors, depending on the person's mood, state of mind, and, more importantly, state of health. According to the therapy practiced, and the observations of the therapist, appropriate treatments can be given to the physical body, or to the energy body itself. That such treatments can be highly effective is attested to by literally thousands of seemingly miraculous cures.

Yet another way of seeing the body's energetic nature is through its chakras. An Eastern concept known as the colored "seven centers," used by many healers, chakras are the points of focus of various levels of energy along the spine, neck, and head. A balance between them is seen as necessary for good health. Their particular color components will be covered in detail in later pages, along with a process for recharging these etheric patterns.

Thus, color healing, as it is described in this book, both comes from and is an important part of the entire realm of energy healing. In the following pages you will discover how it works and how you can use it in many areas of your life to bring a higher state of well-being: auras, color visualization, food and drink, lighting and chromotherapy, and intuitive assessment are all ways of engaging color to heal on the energy level.

RIGHT
The ten body zones for color acupressure.

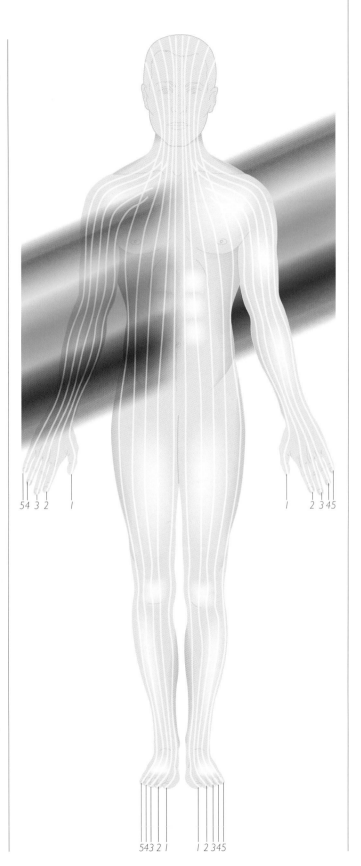

The Aura

THE WORDS "AURA" and "color" are inevitably associated. For those able to see or perceive auras, they almost always appear in various colors. The colors have meanings, depending on where they are located in relation to the body. The meanings tend to vary somewhat, depending on which authority is being consulted. To some degree, every "seer" of auras will, with experience, develop their own interpretations of what they see.

What is an aura, exactly? Most definitions state that it is an energy field surrounding the body of a person, animal, or even an inanimate object. Sensitives say that this energy field emanates from within and is projected out from the body or object, and that it encompasses the physical, mental, emotional, and spiritual levels of being. The aura is made up of a number of layers of energy, each progressively denser the closer it gets to the body. The aura may extend up to three feet or farther from the body. It can likewise be seen as a shimmering mist moving around the exterior of the person, or even as puffballs of colored light escaping from the skin. It also appears as shafts of white, dark, or colored light streaming out from the body. Each of the chakras (see pages 98–99) has its equivalent energy level represented in the aura.

The health of the person under observation can be judged on the purity of the colors. Vibrant, clear colors are a sign of health; dull, muddied colors are indicative of poor health. Disease often shows as black patches or spots, usually in the area where it is present in the physical body. Often the seer will have a strong intuitive sense of where the problem is specifically located if the aura overall is dark.

Emotional states also present colors in the aura; but unlike disease, unless treated, these colors pass as the emotional state changes. Reds and blacks are often associated with anger; a greenish-brown usually indicates jealousy; and gray can suggest depression and fear. Other, more permanent colors are seen to emanate from certain types of personalities: orange from the proud and ambitious person; crimson from those with a passionate, loving nature; yellow from the intellectual; dark blue from the very spiritual; and light blue from those possessing noble ideals. Other, less flattering, personality

BELOW LEFT
Seeing auric purple could suggest that self-empowerment is at hand; orange will encourage the necessary changes.

BELOW RIGHT
The combination of red and green indicates a woman who does too much for others at the expense of herself.

traits also have their commonly seen colors: dull brown from the avaricious; grayish-green from the cunning and deceitful; and grayish-brown from the selfish. A clear green indicates a talented healer.

No matter what front the outer person puts on, the aura reveals the inner truth of that person. All of us have a sensitivity to the emanations of others, whether we are conscious of it or not. Thus, when we meet someone who we instinctively sense is not what they seem, in part at least, we are reading their aura. Our so-called "invisible" auras always go before us and greet each other before we do so on the conscious plane.

Seeing Auras

In a simple exercise to start consciously seeing auras, begin by looking just to the side of the head of the person you are working with. Allow your eyes to go out of focus. The first thing most people see is a light gray or silver band an inch or two wide, surrounding the head. This relates to the electrical processes of the body. If you can recognize this emanation, then you are a seer. Even in this layer you can begin to get information about the person's state of health. Bright, light gray says the person is in generally good health; black or slate gray indicates a depleted energy state. If this is seen, introduce red by one

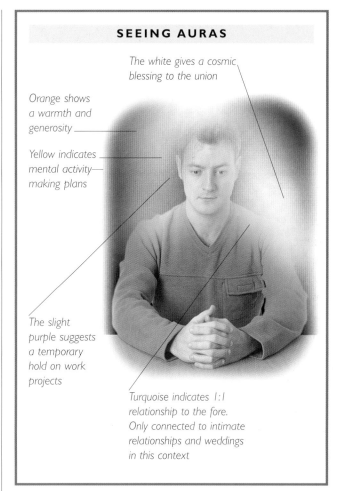

SEEING AURAS

The white gives a cosmic blessing to the union

Orange shows a warmth and generosity

Yellow indicates mental activity—making plans

The slight purple suggests a temporary hold on work projects

Turquoise indicates 1:1 relationship to the fore. Only connected to intimate relationships and weddings in this context

of the methods discussed in this book, to boost the system. Beginners trying to see the aura will find it easier if the person is against a white background.

Within the aura, you may also sense disturbances in the area of one or more of the chakras. If necessary, boost the chakra energy using the method given in Color Balancing the Chakras (see pages 98–99). Your personal way of seeing auras takes practice. Colors will eventually appear, although many people will not see them visually, but will "sense" them. For further color information on auras, use the material in Chapter 2. Good seeing!

LEFT
Green suggests the ability of a healer, with the turquoise implying a need to heal himself first.

ABOVE
An aura interpretation at a crossroads in life can give clear indications of the appropriate path to follow.

Color Balancing the Chakras

THE CHAKRAS ARE the seven points in the body where energy is focused. The main chakras are positioned from the base of the spine up to the crown of the head, although there are many other chakra points throughout the body. The whole concept of chakras and energy focus is part of an understanding that the mind, body, and spirit exist as part of a field of energy, the energy of the earth and the cosmos; yet, within that field of energy, it exists as an individual being in its own right. Various religions and philosophies give names to these different yet interconnected levels and dimensions of energy. If energy comes in many

shapes and forms, heat, light, inertia, momentum, and so on, then the idea follows that we, as physical, mental, emotional, and spiritual beings, embody many different levels of energy that we can consciously control through appropriate means.

CHAKRA	GLANDS	COLOR	
Crown chakra	Pineal		PURPLE
Brow chakra	Pituitary		INDIGO
Throat chakra	Thyroid		BLUE
Heart chakra	Thymus		GREEN
Solar plexus chakra	Spleen		YELLOW
Sacral chakra	Adrenals		ORANGE
Root chakra	Ovaries/testes		RED

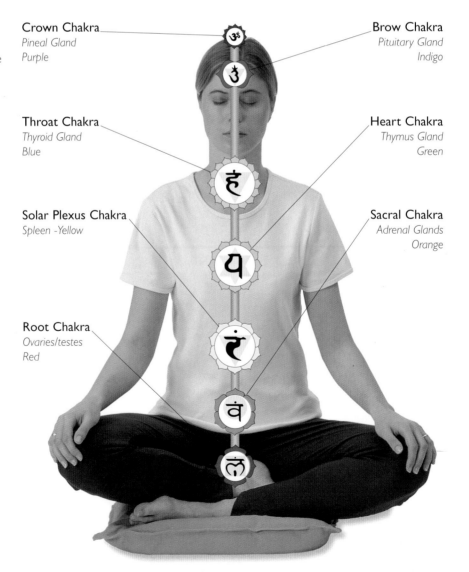

RIGHT
The arrangement of the chakras along the spine, and their corresponding colors and glands.

Crown Chakra
Pineal Gland
Purple

Brow Chakra
Pituitary Gland
Indigo

Throat Chakra
Thyroid Gland
Blue

Heart Chakra
Thymus Gland
Green

Solar Plexus Chakra
Spleen -Yellow

Sacral Chakra
Adrenal Glands
Orange

Root Chakra
Ovaries/testes
Red

Within the levels of energy we embody there exists a "spectrum" of energies, not unlike, and in fact related to, color. At its extremes are the denser, purely physical energies that relate to the world of matter and reproduction, related to red and often described as "dense." At the "highest" level are the energies of the spirit: lighter, subtle, refined, easily overlooked in the hurly-burly of everyday life, and related to purple. Between these are five other levels, each relating to a different facet of life. The energies of red, orange, and yellow are considered coarser, with the energies of blue, indigo, and purple more ethereal. In the middle, and neutral, is green. Each of these levels relates to an organ of the body, and has a corresponding color. The colors follow the spectrum, with the longest, slowest wavelength of red connected to the lowest level of body energy. The connections continue upward, with purple representing the faster, highest spiritual energies.

The position of the chakras is shown in the accompanying chart, and the colors and their corresponding glands are shown opposite. The spine chakras also embody various human attributes, which can be strengthened or given emphasis through raising the energy of the associated chakra. The associated attributes are:

RED root chakra: sexuality, survival, reproduction

ORANGE sacral chakra: "gut level" emotion, creativity

YELLOW solar plexus chakra: self-esteem, relationships, social identity

GREEN heart chakra: love, self-acceptance, acceptance of others

BLUE throat chakra: self-expression, voicing opinions

INDIGO brow chakra: intuition, insight

PURPLE crown chakra: cosmic connection, spiritual opening, and understanding.

ENERGIZING THE SPINAL CHAKRAS

The chakras are often described as a rotating wheel or vortex of energy, and in the following exercise, you may find it helpful to visualize them as such.

Because of the powerful connection between colors and the chakras, by applying the appropriate color, their functioning is improved and balanced. This principle can be used to give an overall boost to the system, to focus healing on a specific area of the body, or to strengthen the dimension of life associated with a particular chakra. The method is simplicity itself.

1. Close your eyes and visualize the color corresponding to the chakra you wish to enliven.

2. Now place both hands over your eyes and visualize that particular color flowing into the palms of your hands and energizing them.

3. Place both hands over the chakra area down the front of the body and visualize the color flowing into the body, directing the color through to the spinal chakra point.

4. Repeat the same procedure for any or all of the remaining chakras, usually for three minutes at a time, to align, restore, harmonize, and balance, as desired.

LEFT
Energizing the chakras can be accomplished with a simple hands-on visualization technique.

Chromotherapy: Color Projection

THE ANCIENT EGYPTIANS, Babylonians, and Assyrians have bequeathed us a legacy which is as powerful today as it was then: chromotherapy, the therapy of bathing all or part of the body in colored light. The colors used corresponded with those that disease caused in the body: yellow jaundice, blue lips, fever-red skin. Because the ancients had no means of separating the colors of the spectrum, they used naturally colored materials. Particularly prized were transparent stones in intense colors. Yellow beryls were used for jaundice, bloodstone for hemorrhage, and lapis lazuli for the blue of restricted circulation. Diamond was considered a cure-all, prized for its brilliance. Other colored materials were also used: flowers and plants, white oil, red lead, red ocher, black lizards, and indigo. Verdigris, a green copper carbonate, was mixed with wax to treat cataracts.

As colored glass became available in the last centuries BCE, the emphasis in colored light shifted to this man-made substance, and stones became more valued as items of adornment, while still maintaining the mystique from their days of healing. The places of healing also shifted from temples to churches, where the stained glass windows swamped the congregation with healing light.

The principle involved in the modern practice of chromotherapy is simple, and it is something that can easily be carried out at home. Using different colored gels or slides with a light source, you can either bathe or pinpoint the body with the appropriate healing color. This can be done through the use of high-powered lamps acquired from theater supply stores, colored bulbs, or even with a flashlight. At home, colored glass can be placed in front of a window, or, if too expensive,

The ancients considered diamond a cure-all, prized for its brilliance.

cellophane can be used—although glass is better. The choice of color is guided by the healing applications outlined in Chapter 2, and in the list of specific ailments in the color acupressure section (see pages 108–113).

For the best results from chromotherapy, it is advisable to go to a qualified color practitioner, but it can also be applied at home. There are several general principles in its use that are important to keep in mind.

1. The recipient of the treatment can either lie down or sit in a chair, with the lamp directed toward them.

2. The exposure time should be limited to no more than 10 minutes at any one session.

3. Certain colors have specific limits on their use: red must never be applied to anyone with a heart condition; never apply purple to the face, always apply it to the back of the head.

Other cautions are listed under the information for the specific color in Chapter 2.

If a treatment is overdone—the person has an agitated reaction and feels uncomfortable—flood them with green light for a few minutes to neutralize, dilute, and clear the previous application.

4. Treat conditions that affect the whole body, such as flu or colds, by flooding. Treat conditions affecting specific areas, such as a damaged knee or sprained elbow, by pinpointing, focusing the color on the affected area only.

Experience a treatment of colored light for maximum health and well-being.

The use of colored glass in church windows was an early form of chromotherapy, bathing the congregation in color.

Cosmic Colored Breathing Techniques

BREATH IS THE vital force that sustains life. The very air we breathe is full of brilliant light and colors. To practice color breathing in a deep, rhythmic way, visualize the colored rays coming from the sun's life force. While absorbing large quantities of pure air we raise our bodily vibrations, which in turn encourages vitality and a healthy mind and body. Color breathing has been used successfully for centuries for health and healing, and for the purpose of support in our daily activities.

When practicing the following techniques always remember to breathe in through the nose and out through the mouth.

COSMIC PURPLE BREATH

This breathing technique will allow you to go walkabout into the universe. It is a splendid way of harnessing life's energy force of breath to move you into the celestial realms. This process of breath control encourages you with each expansion and contraction to move more fully into this life, allowing you to stay in the moment.

Stage One: In Breath

1. Lie down and focus on your own natural breathing, imagining the air filled with violet-purple.

2. Hold the next in-breath and explore the space where you have stopped. Dare to move into this U-bend place, if only for a few seconds.

Stage Two: Out Breath

3. Release your breath and on completion of expelling the air, wait in this place of turning around to see where it leads you, before you fill your lungs again.

RIGHT
Color breathing techniques can infuse you with new life and vigor.

BRILLIANT RAINBOW OXYGENATION BREATHING

This is a life-enhancing technique that increases the purity of the blood through the breath. It can be practiced at any time, anywhere, and incorporates all the rainbow colors of brilliance into the system. Before starting, focus on a clear quartz crystal or a diamond—or even a glass of water—to encourage the brilliance to penetrate the psyche.

1. Sitting or lying down with the shoulders and body relaxed, fill your lungs with a full breath and hold it for as long as you can.

2. Holding the breath, slowly count from one upward and see how far you can go before you have to release the breath.

3. Repeat the exercise three times in a row and arrive at your maximum number. The desired count to reach is 50, when your system will be fully energized. Do not despair if you only attain a low number. It just shows you need to work with the process. Practice the technique once a day and continue for life, so that you are constantly recharging yourself with life's supreme, brilliant balance.

Golden Breath of Trust

GOLDEN SURRENDER TEST

Use this process to see how trusting you are of the universe. When you can trust, you can surrender yourself to the delights of the cosmos.

Take a full breath in and release it. Note if the breath going out is shorter than the breath taken in. If it is, then it shows that somewhere along the way you have lost faith in life, maybe as a child experiencing disappointment, shock or criticism. The subconscious eventually learns never to trust the universe to supply the next breath, so a tendency develops to grab the next incoming breath quickly—just in case the universe forgets.

THE GOLDEN YELLOW REMEDY

This technique will enable you to surrender to gold's delight and success, by releasing past fears and hurts. Visualize an exquisite golden haze that colors the air you breathe. Each time you breathe out, consciously extend the out-breath, encouraging it to lengthen. Pause for four counts before you begin a new intake of breath. You may experience fear—or even panic—but realize you are now in control.

Living Color Breathing

Be aware that daily activities can be enhanced by incorporating colored breathing. Choose the appropriate color, allowing the air around you to be filled with it, or even just think about it. Take deep breaths in, hold the color for a second, and release it. As an example, turquoise breathing can be used to steady the nerves before entering the boardroom, or for that important interview. Even think pink into your breath when faced with a mugger! All colors can be used to help ease the daily round of living. Look to the healing uses in Chapter 2 to discover the color to use.

BELOW
Our own breathing is a constant reminder of our connection to the living world around us.

Foods for Color Healing

COLOR IS AN essential food and color starvation is a most distressing condition. Color balance is as necessary for us as nutritional balance, or air for our lungs. We are sensitive to the color of foods, because color cues our body as to which nutrients a specific food contains. The color tells us which food has the nutrients we need. There is an essential connection between the vibration rate that a particular color has and the pattern of nutrients a particular food provides. The appetite will be increased or decreased by its color.

Different-colored foods taken into the body can be used to heal, lift the mood, and stimulate health. Food can be disharmonious with our body rhythm, causing indigestion, heartburn, and general imbalance to occur within the system. The preferred foods are those organically grown with no additives—this keeps the color vibration alive. Microwaved, processed, and junk foods are dead foods: their color energy has been removed.

ABOVE

Red foods can act as a pick-me-up, restoring zest, energy, and drive.

BENEFICIAL FOOD COLORS

Generally, red, orange, and yellow foods are hot and stimulating. Green foods are alkaline, promote balance within the body, and are a tonic for the system. Blue, indigo, and purple foods soothe and cool. More specifically:

● **RED** These foods lift energy and dissipate lethargy and tiredness. They quicken the bloodflow and expand the arteries.

● **ORANGE** Optimism and change are characteristic benefits of orange foods, which also help lift grief and disappointment. Orange foods eliminate stagnant food from the gut and strengthen the immune system.

● **YELLOW** Laughter, joy, and fun are encouraged, and depression is lifted. The natural laxative, yellow foods eliminate all unwanted toxins and feed the central nervous system.

● **GREEN** The green, chlorophyll foods improve physical stamina and alleviate apprehension, panic, fear, and nausea. Herbs are a tonic for the entire system.

● **BLUE** Blue foods help concentration and heal anxiety. Peace and relaxation are the gifts of blue foods. They also strengthen capillaries and help to lower blood pressure.

● **INDIGO** Foods of this color bring relief from insecurity. They help to put structure back into one's life. They promote growth of new tissue, and alleviate eczema and bruising.

● **PURPLE** Purple foods promote leadership, and calm the emotionally erratic. They are beneficial for mental disorders, the eyes, and the activation of spiritual awareness.

SOLARIZED WATER

Solarized water is a sun-charged drink. This method of drinking liquid sunshine can be taken at any time, and can be incorporated with other healing methods.

To create it, you need a clear glass full of pure water, and a strip or strips of colored cellophane wide enough to cover the glass. Refer to Chapter 2 to find out which color to use. Wrap the cellophane around the glass and secure with tape. Place the glass on a window ledge so that it gets at least 30 minutes of direct sunlight. The longer the exposure, the stronger the color infusion will be. The effects of treatment with solarized water are slow in coming—but they will occur. When solarizing red, orange, or yellow, always drink the water slowly. Do not take yellow water after 6 p.m. as it can be too energizing before bedtime, or on the bladder!

LEFT
Use solarized water to drink in sun-charged color energy.

ABOVE
Yellow foods bring in the sunshine, releasing depression and clearing the system of toxins.

Weight Loss and Gain

The subject of food inevitably brings up the question of weight loss or gain. Color can be helpful here too. To reduce excess weight the color to use is yellow. This color is one that hates to carry excess baggage. It promotes agility both of mind and body, so wear it when exercising to keep you moving and pepped up. Or you can eat it as yellow food, drink it as solarized water, or as yellow fruit juice. Also visualize and incorporate yellow breathing.

Blue, on the other hand is the color to encourage weight gain. Blue inhibits activity, allowing the calories to gather and put on flesh. Psychologically, it does everything quietly and with discretion, creating the right emotional environment needed for your body to be given the chance to increase itself. Again, wear it, eat it, drink it, visualize it, or use the blue-colored breath technique.

Music and Color

MUSIC AND COLOR both have the ability to make profound changes in body chemistry. The brain responds to each, and in turn affects hormone levels, and even the strength of the immune system. They are both vibrations, and vibrations can harm or heal, equally.

Testing Yourself with Music and Color

All musical notes and body organs relate to a color. To check for any discrepancies in the system, note first the Color Music Guide. This simple music scale shows its equivalent color and body part.

To do a quick self-assessment, sit or stand and take in a deep breath. Sing all the notes of the scale from the top to the bottom. You can sing the notes on the "ah" sound if preferred. Be conscious of any note that sounds weak, or on which you falter, which indicates a weakness in that area.

Healing with Music

A basic rule using music as a healing therapy is to remember that the higher up the scale the note, the higher up the body it has an effect. Start at the midriff, the yellow/E. All conditions affecting the bowel and lower intestines incorporate the notes of C, D, and E, with heavy music such as Wagner. Problems higher up the body work from the midriff upward, with the colored notes of G, A, and B, using lighter music such as the Nutcracker Suite. Play appropriate music for whichever end, using moderate music for the midriff area.

The Healing Rainbow

You can take yourself on a rainbow journey: just select four pieces of appropriate music and relax in a chair, visualizing the following as you play your selections—music that:

1. Reminds you of walking along a seashore;

2. Music to climb up white cliffs by the beach;

3. Music to climb down the opposite side of the cliff to a beautiful turquoise lagoon below; and finally:

4. Music for gently easing yourself into the lagoon, enabling you to wade into the lagoon to stand under a cosmic cascading waterfall. There, select a colored crystal from the depths below.

Recall any feelings, images, or colors that you have experienced on this healing rainbow journey. Use the interpretations in Chapter 2, The Psychology of Color, to interpret any colors you see.

The sea and beach represent your emotional life; the ascent up the cliffs your childhood; the descent is your current life situation and your aspirations; the lagoon is your true self and desires. The rainbow shower is a cleansing purifier, and the choice of crystal color is the key to your next step in life.

To obtain an in-depth cassette recording of the above with specially chosen music, and with more details to interpret your images and colors, see Useful Addresses on page 142 for *The Healing Rainbow* tape.

COLOR MUSIC GUIDE		
COLOR	MUSICAL NOTE	BODY RELATIONSHIP
RED	C	genitals, blood, legs, muscles
ORANGE	D	kidneys, intestines, lower abdomen
YELLOW	E	liver, gallbladder, pancreas, stomach
GREEN	F	heart, shoulders, lower lungs
BLUE	G	throat, base of the skull, upper lungs
INDIGO	A	skeleton, eyes, sinuses
PURPLE	B	brain, scalp, crown of the head

RIGHT
Visualize a cascading waterfall on the musical rainbow path to renewal and enlightenment.

Color Yourself Well with Color Acupressure

COLOR ACUPRESSURE can be used at any time and anywhere. With the help of color acupressure techniques you can be your own healer: this treatment is self-administered. With an instant, on-the-spot application, you can bring relief from pain and start to eliminate discomforts and illness.

All the organs of the body are mirrored in the hands. Stimulating certain centers on the hands has a direct energy link to various parts of the body, and can bring about healing. Similar to a telephone, you simply pick up the hand-piece and dial, pressing a point to send a message along an unseen wire to the intended destination. Acupressure gives the meridian-related body part a gentle kick-start, a boost of energy. It is simply a matter of putting pressure on the trigger spot. Acupressure is a drug-free method of increasing the blood flow to these areas so that the body can restore itself to renewed health. There are pressure zones all over

the body; the hands have been chosen here because of their convenience. The pressure points can be compared with receptors, taking in information and relaying it inwardly through the body.

As man lives in an ocean of color, bathed continually in its vibration, it is beneficial to harness this energy at the same time as applying acupressure. The seven colors of the spectrum are used for this. By introducing a healing color as part of the process, we work on the psyche, affecting the brain, which in turn directs the body to heal itself. The color becomes your subconscious counselor. To the effect of the color is added an affirmation, the "color counseling sentence," to begin counteracting the deeply held belief that underlies the complaint. Affirmations are powerful in their own right, and when combined with color and acupressure, add an extra dimension to healing.

RIGHT
Color acupressure is a simple and powerful tool of self-healing.

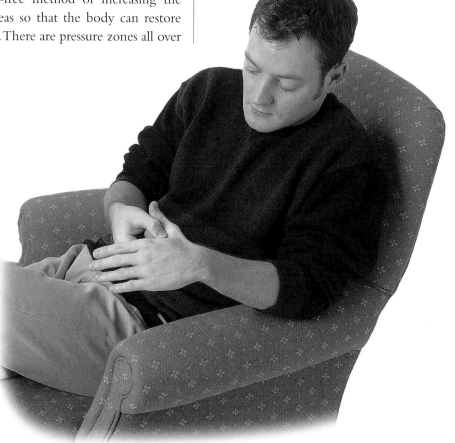

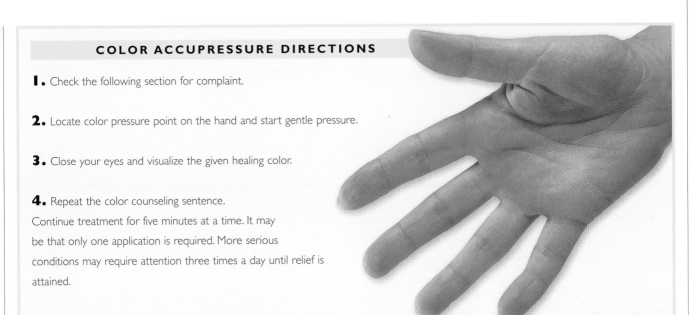

COLOR ACCUPRESSURE DIRECTIONS

1. Check the following section for complaint.

2. Locate color pressure point on the hand and start gentle pressure.

3. Close your eyes and visualize the given healing color.

4. Repeat the color counseling sentence.
Continue treatment for five minutes at a time. It may
be that only one application is required. More serious
conditions may require attention three times a day until relief is
attained.

AILMENT/CONDITION HEALING COLOR	COUNSELING / REPEAT HEALING AFFIRMATION
Acne *Healing Color:* Yellow	The world is large enough to fulfill my needs. I expand with joy.
AIDS *Healing Color:* Green	I am magnificent and free from guilt.
Alzheimer's disease *Healing Color:* Purple	I can be here and not feel fear. Life is perfect for me.
Angina *Healing Color:* Green	I will release and relax and allow a joyous rhythm to consume me.

AILMENT/CONDITION HEALING COLOR	COUNSELING / REPEAT HEALING AFFIRMATION
Anorexia *Healing Color:* Yellow	I am a full bloom rose of sweet scent and perfection.
Asthma *Healing Color:* Orange	I will not help others at the expense of myself. I am gloriously free.
Breast problems *Healing Color:* Indigo	I am beautiful and magnificent as a woman, a wonder to behold.
Bronchitis *Healing Color:* Indigo	My internal freeways are clear. I experience love riding along life's highways.

AILMENT/CONDITION HEALING COLOR	COUNSELING / REPEAT HEALING AFFIRMATION
Bunions *Healing Color: Orange*	I surmount any obstacles that come my way. Rejoice in the constant care I give myself. I can consider myself a part of life's richness.
Motion sickness *Healing Color: Green*	While traveling I shall take each second one at a time. I am safe from one second to another.
Catarrh *Healing Color: Orange*	I shall loosen up and allow myself space to be content.
Back problems *Healing Color: Indigo*	I will not hold myself back. Every day and in every way I grow stronger and stronger.
Boils *Healing Color: Yellow*	I can empty my life of all that does not agree with me. I am full of the spirit of peace.
Bowel problems *Healing Color: Yellow*	As I let go of the old, so the new can come in. Whatever the world presents to me I am ready.
Common cold *Healing Color: Green*	There is time to make a space for all I need and want to do. I will focus and center myself.

AILMENT/CONDITION HEALING COLOR	COUNSELING / REPEAT HEALING AFFIRMATION
Cystitis *Healing Color: Yellow*	I feel strong as I stand my ground. I am a very important part of this universe.
Deafness *Healing Color: Yellow*	I will only allow sweet music to mine ears. Celestial tones to calm my being.
Depression *Healing Color: Yellow*	Live, love, laugh, and be happy. I can be loved for ever and for ever.
Diabetes *Healing Color: Yellow*	The world is mine—my make, and I glorify life's sweet opportunities.
Diarrhea *Healing Color: Indigo*	I appreciate holding on to that which has been given me. I accept with love and gratitude.
Dyslexia *Healing Color: Yellow*	I am unique and different. Full of original wisdom and joy. Brilliance is my aim.
Ear problems *Healing Color: Yellow*	I can untie the chains and let a balance return to me. Power is gentle and true.

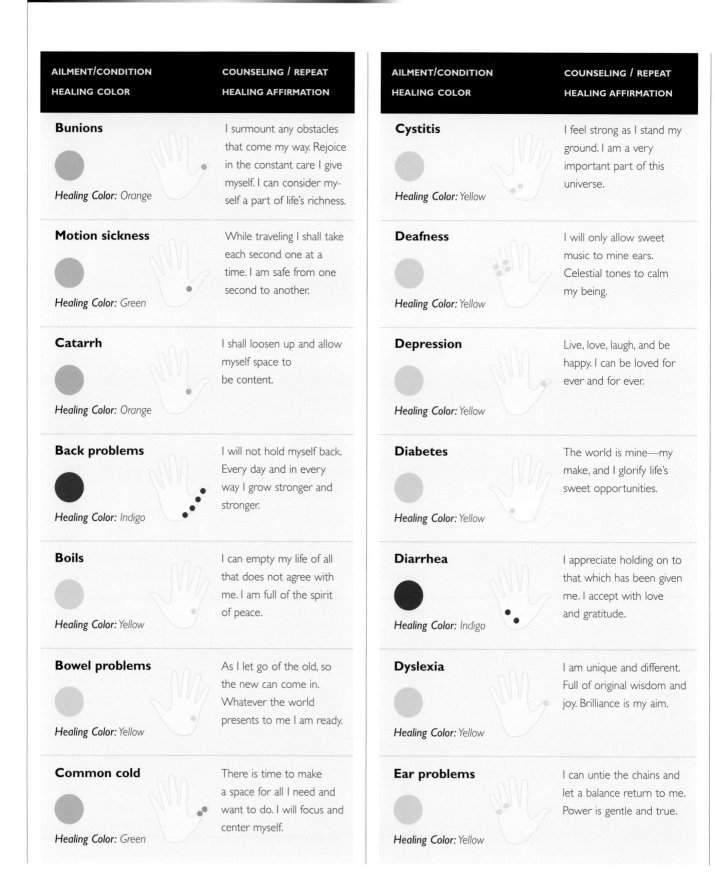

AILMENT/CONDITION HEALING COLOR	COUNSELING / REPEAT HEALING AFFIRMATION

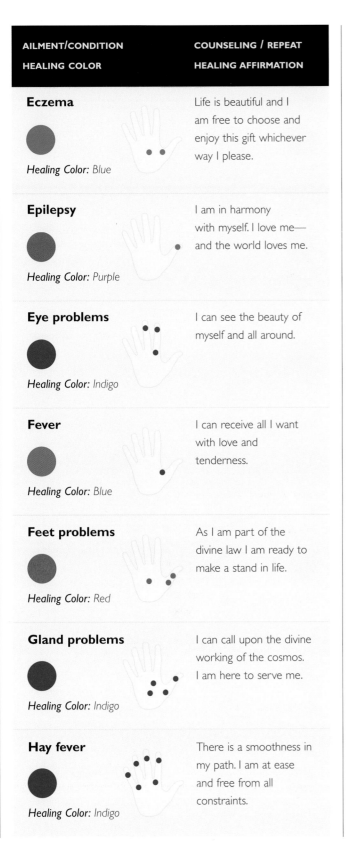

Eczema

Healing Color: *Blue*

Life is beautiful and I am free to choose and enjoy this gift whichever way I please.

Epilepsy

Healing Color: *Purple*

I am in harmony with myself. I love me—and the world loves me.

Eye problems

Healing Color: *Indigo*

I can see the beauty of myself and all around.

Fever

Healing Color: *Blue*

I can receive all I want with love and tenderness.

Feet problems

Healing Color: *Red*

As I am part of the divine law I am ready to make a stand in life.

Gland problems

Healing Color: *Indigo*

I can call upon the divine working of the cosmos. I am here to serve me.

Hay fever

Healing Color: *Indigo*

There is a smoothness in my path. I am at ease and free from all constraints.

AILMENT/CONDITION HEALING COLOR	COUNSELING / REPEAT HEALING AFFIRMATION

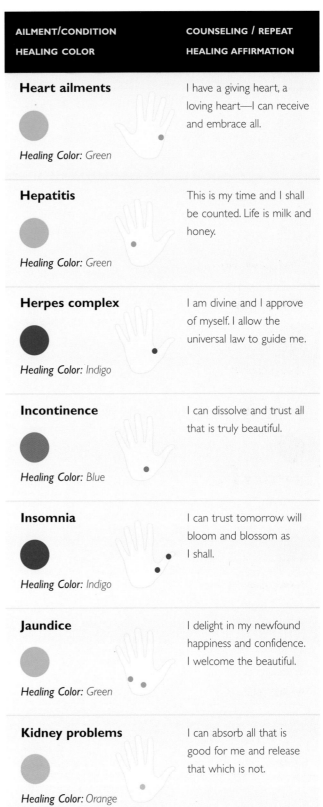

Heart ailments

Healing Color: *Green*

I have a giving heart, a loving heart—I can receive and embrace all.

Hepatitis

Healing Color: *Green*

This is my time and I shall be counted. Life is milk and honey.

Herpes complex

Healing Color: *Indigo*

I am divine and I approve of myself. I allow the universal law to guide me.

Incontinence

Healing Color: *Blue*

I can dissolve and trust all that is truly beautiful.

Insomnia

Healing Color: *Indigo*

I can trust tomorrow will bloom and blossom as I shall.

Jaundice

Healing Color: *Green*

I delight in my newfound happiness and confidence. I welcome the beautiful.

Kidney problems

Healing Color: *Orange*

I can absorb all that is good for me and release that which is not.

AILMENT / CONDITION HEALING COLOR	COUNSELING / REPEAT HEALING AFFIRMATION
Knee troubles *Healing Color: Orange*	I can move with ease and grace. I have no fear, life is full of wonderful experience.
Liver complaints *Healing Color: Green*	My spirit is peaceful. I trust whatever the cosmos supplies, I am clean and pure.
Menopause *Healing Color: Orange*	I can, with ease, release the old and let the new become my teacher. I am constantly recycled through love.
Menstrual pain *Healing Color: Indigo*	I can rejoice at the universal flow of life. I am constantly reminded of my magnificence.
Migraine *Healing Color: Indigo*	I am free from restriction. I can plan only the very best for myself. I am loved.
Nausea *Healing Color: Green*	I can have and hold the nutrients of goodness from this life. I trust the process of regeneration.
Nervous disorders *Healing Color: Yellow*	I communicate and hold council with the self. I acknowledge all parts of me.

AILMENT / CONDITION HEALING COLOR	COUNSELING / REPEAT HEALING AFFIRMATION
Ovary problems *Healing Color: Red*	I trust my intuitiveness. I delight in my expression of creativeness. I can follow my spiritual path into eternity.
Overweight *Healing Color: Red*	No need to hide from life's joys. I can enjoy the rich pattern that is set out especially for me.
Pain *Healing Color: Indigo*	I will listen to hidden messages of self-knowing that are given to me. I am ready and alert to following my path free of pain. I prefer pleasure.
Phlebitis *Healing Color: Green*	I will let go and let faith decide my future moves whichever way I go— I go with blessings and inner peace.
Phobias *Healing Color: Orange*	I trust that whatever comes my way, I shall be supported with the universe's divine presence.
Pneumonia *Healing Color: Indigo*	I create my own safety. My heart is filled with hope and joy at life's opportunities.
Psoriasis *Healing Color: Orange*	I love myself just as I am. I can feel only love and kindness embracing me.

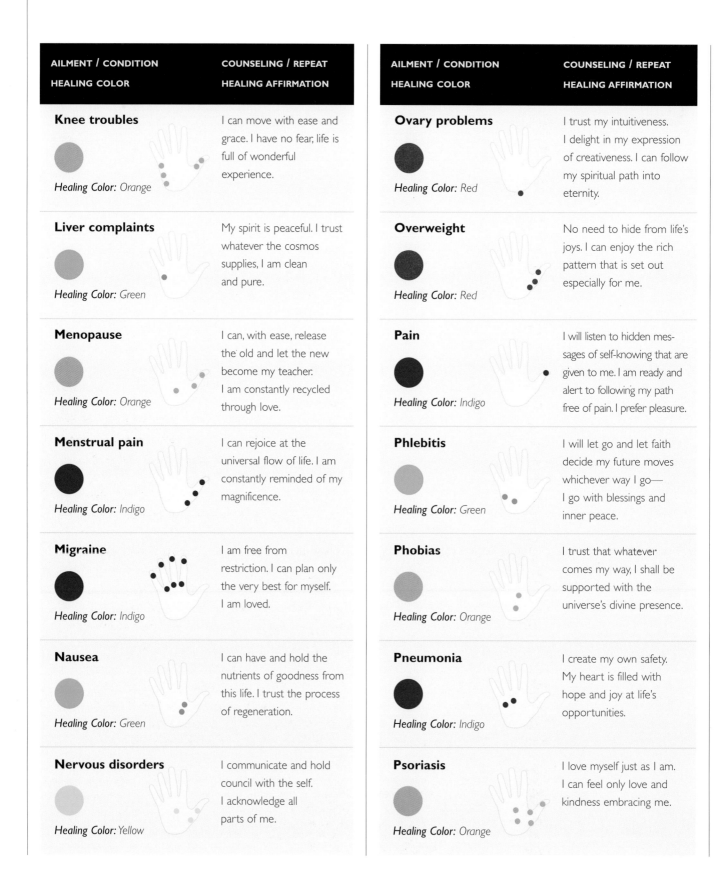

AILMENT / CONDITION HEALING COLOR	COUNSELING / REPEAT HEALING AFFIRMATION
Quinsy (throat abscess) *Healing Color: Indigo*	I can follow my heart and speak my mind. I can hear only the murmuring of gentle loving.
Rashes *Healing Color: Yellow*	I can now move beyond past limitations. I am free to choose and trust the process of life.
Rheumatism *Healing Color: Blue*	I can follow freely my own inner sound of knowing. I have the power to accept the best for myself.
Sinus problems *Healing Color: Indigo*	I love that little child that is within me. I love him/her and will nurture him/her forever.
Snoring *Healing Color: Indigo*	There is a right time and a right place for everything. I give myself permission to be heard in the fullness of the light.
Sprains *Healing Color: Orange*	It it safe for me to be flexible, I rejoice in change and the new. I trust the process of life will support me.
Stiff neck *Healing Color: Yellow*	It is safe for me to venture out into life. There are more ways than one to endless joy.

AILMENT / CONDITION HEALING COLOR	COUNSELING / REPEAT HEALING AFFIRMATION
Teeth problems *Healing Color: Blue*	The goodness of life belongs to me. I can break down all I receive into sustenance of love and joy.
Thrush *Healing Color: Green*	I love and delight in my femininity. I am the pathway to paradise.
Varicose veins *Healing Color: Indigo*	My life's blood is free to travel in safety and joy.
Venereal disease *Healing Color: Red*	I trust the process of life and rejoice in my divine gift of exquisite pleasure through my sexuality.
Water retention *Healing Color: Yellow*	Life is full and plenty. I can release knowing the universe will provide.
Warts *Healing Color: Orange*	Everything about me is divine. The universe accepts and embraces all of me.
Wisdom teeth *Healing Color: Yellow*	I can go forth and will enjoy all my glorious potential.
Womb problems *Healing Color: Purple*	I can carry the love of the world with ease and pride. My cup is full.

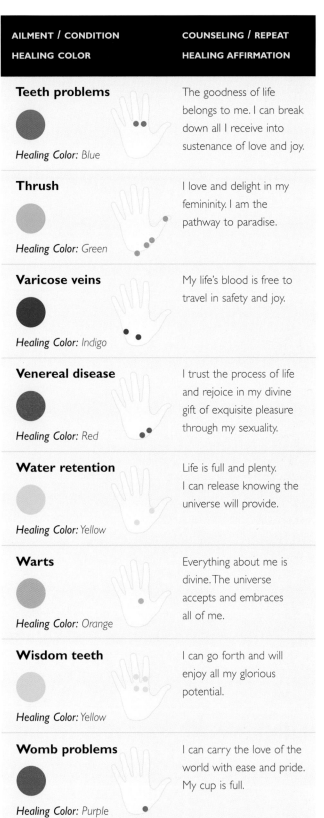

Color and Crystals

THE MINERAL KINGDOM IS ultimately the foundation for all life, both on Earth and beyond. A special state of mineral matter, in the form of crystals, is all around us. Crystals or crystalline matter are part of our living body; we eat crystals; we use them a hundred times a day in all their various forms. In the past two decades, we have experienced the growth of "crystal consciousness"—an awareness of the life of the mineral kingdom.

Color is one of most neglected properties of crystals. It is inbuilt into the structure of crystals; in fact, into the very atoms from which crystals are made. Color is one of the ways in which crystals perfectly balance their own internal energies. This inbuilt color energy, and its interchange, is demonstrated daily in chemistry classes: silvery potassium, when placed in a flame, burns lilac; copper burns green; and white strontium burns red. These are but a few examples, and clearly demonstrate color interaction. Not only natural crystals, but even a laboratory-derived crystal or one home-grown from a kit will still resonate to its color content, even if the structure is not purely nature's own—if it wasn't perfect in its own right, it wouldn't be a crystal.

LEFT

Potassium placed in a flame produces blue-colored light.

RIGHT

The combination of natural crystals with color provides us with a powerful tool for healing.

From the standpoint of energy healing, colored crystals are the very archetypes we are seeking. There is much written about "crystal healing"; inevitably there is a list of illnesses and crystals that are supposed to heal them. But what is rarely noticed is that a very large portion of these are *color* healing properties.

ABOVE

The pink color of rose quartz offers consistency of affection, and universal harmony.

In an earlier section, auras were discussed. They are part of the whole field of energy that makes up the human being, and are part of the reason that energy healing is possible. Part of the auric makeup is the projection of our own consciousness. When crystals are brought into the aura, they interact with it. But what do they do? Essentially, the crystal does nothing more than mirror what is already there—your whole makeup, including some things you might not be aware of. Within each and every one of us—more deeply buried in some than in others—is the ability to heal, to bring about a state of perfect balance and harmony at all levels. The crystal is an archetype of perfect balance and harmony. Thus we recognize in the crystal that which already exists within us. We couldn't recognize it if it wasn't already within us. But many mistakenly believe that what we experience in the crystal belongs to the crystal, rather than to us—so out of touch are many of us with those dimensions of ourselves. So the crystal is perceived as giving off healing energy, when what we are really experiencing is our own ability reflected back to us. Because many of those inner dimensions are intimately linked to color, the use of crystals in combination with color becomes a very powerful tool for creating understanding and inner harmony—called healing. The impact of the color coming from within the stone will act as a guide into many avenues of color consciousness. How then can we put the combination of crystals and color to work for us?

Choosing a Crystal Color

A common concern is choosing the correct crystal. The truth is, there is no perfect stone for everyone. All crystals have their own worth, their own messages and experiences to be encountered. It will help you to resolve the dilemma when faced with a selection of stones to just pick up the one that most attracts you—often the first one your eye is drawn to. For that matter, just close your eyes and pick one up—your instincts will invariably be correct. Even if you get the "wrong" one, no harm can come of it. If you are choosing a crystal for the purpose of touching into your intuitive physic ability, then use your left hand, as this is the side leading to divine power, directly through the heart. Use your right hand to choose a crystal color if you want information relating to your life on a day-to-day basis. The right hand represents physical power and has the ability to push troubles away.

ABOVE
All of nature's rainbow can be found in the Mineral Kingdom.

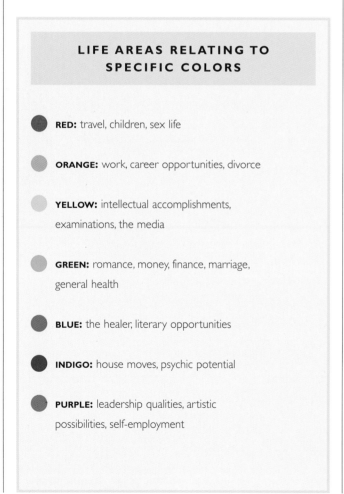

LIFE AREAS RELATING TO SPECIFIC COLORS

- **RED:** travel, children, sex life

- **ORANGE:** work, career opportunities, divorce

- **YELLOW:** intellectual accomplishments, examinations, the media

- **GREEN:** romance, money, finance, marriage, general health

- **BLUE:** the healer, literary opportunities

- **INDIGO:** house moves, psychic potential

- **PURPLE:** leadership qualities, artistic possibilities, self-employment

Using Colored Crystals

THE LAYING-ON OF A CRYSTAL

In this treatment, the crystal may literally be laid on the body of the person receiving treatment, or it may be held just in front or behind the body. Use the Color Acupressure Chart (see pages 109–113) to choose an appropriately colored crystal. Or, refer to the properties of the colors under "physical healing" or "emotional healing" in Chapter 2. Have the person being treated either lie down or sit in a chair. Place the colored crystal on, or hold it over, the afflicted area. In addition to the colored crystal itself, visualize a flow of color going into the area you are treating. If you have only a general idea of where the affliction is located, place the crystal on or over the nearest chakra (see pages 98–99). If treating yourself, use the same procedure. For a general top-up, use a clear quartz crystal to lighten up the system.

The Pendulum Technique

This technique also involves the chakras. Although we cannot see the spinning chakra wheels with the naked eye, it is advisable to keep them balanced and topped up so that they all rotate in rhythm with each other. You can do this by swinging a crystal pendulum over each chakra spot on the body.

One method is to use a clear quartz crystal—embodying brilliance—for the purpose of reviving these energy centers, but to balance and give an extra boost to each chakra individually, you should use a crystal that is the same color as each chakra.

Sit the person being treated—you can treat yourself in the same way—in a chair or have them lie down. Hold your chosen crystal suspended from a chain or piece of string. Let the pendulum swing in front of each chakra in turn, starting at the base and working up. The pendulum may swing wildly at first, turning in either direction. If so, just wait until it settles down and stops, showing that it's balanced. Further information about the use of pendulums is found on pages 124–125.

Seeking Insights

This technique is simplicity itself: all you need to do is hold a crystal of your choice while meditating. Meditation is discussed in greater detail on pages 120–121, but it is nothing more than just sitting quietly with your eyes closed, a period of quiet reflection, and allowing yourself to see whatever comes to you. If you are seeking answers in a particular area of your life, choose a crystal color from the list opposite.

BELOW

Use a crystal pendulum for chakra balancing and healing.

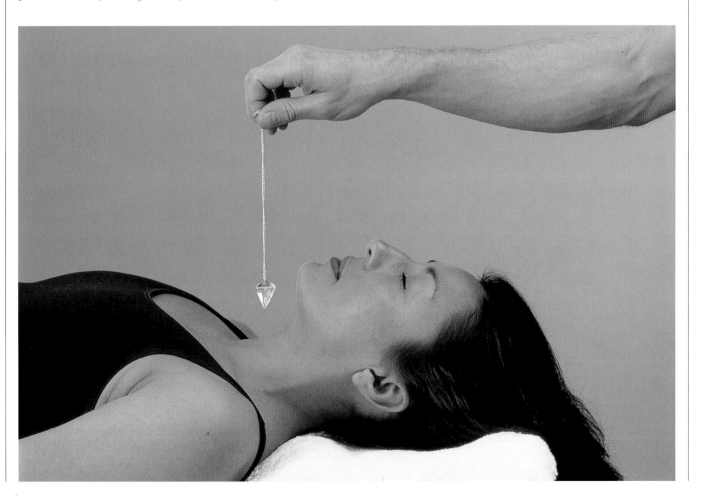

Color Healing for Animals

WHILE WE ARE aware that methods other than conventional medicine can be used to heal the human race, so the same idea is evolving in the world of animal care. All animals with backbones have very sophisticated eyes—often surpassing those of humans—which indicates their receptivity to color. Color therapy is becoming a key element for animal healing, an area in which the author has considerable experience. Animals share a large percentage of the same DNA as humans, and their energy-structure is the same. Responding uninhibitedly as they do to the "truth" of nature, they will relate to the naturalness of color for healing when they are in need.

Healing Approach

Animals are able to sense your intentions and motives. They have a very highly developed sense of perception and need to be treated with respect. That's why they love to attend our meditation sessions—to soak up the energy. Regard each animal as an individual. It is important to allow them to become accustomed to you first. If the animal is walking, then let them come to you. If not, approach them gradually, speaking softly and reassuringly. Do not rush—by your gentleness they will pick up your healing energy. Allow the animal to respond; it may be as little as a movement of the eye. Often an animal will draw attention to the affected area, guiding you to a point of healing.

Timing

Animals know when they have had enough healing. They will either walk away or the healer will sense that the animal has switched off. A ten-minute session once a week is a good general guide, or as many as seems necessary for a very sick animal.

Healing Technique

The healer usually channels energy through the hands. They can be placed either on the animal directly or a short distance away from them. The animal will then take this in-flow of healing energy into itself, boosting its own natural healing.

LEFT
All inhabitants of the Animal Kingdom can benefit from the healing power of color's vibration.

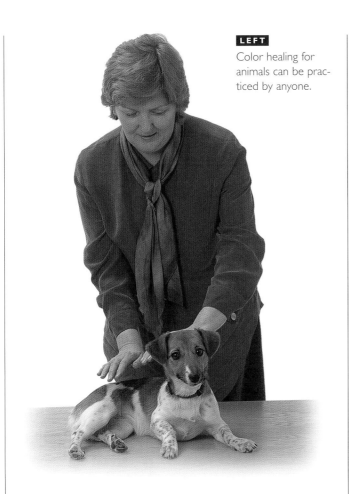

Specific Colors for Specific Ailments

Vertebrate animals can be worked on along the spine using the chakra colors as for a human—the tail end is red, working up to purple at the head (see pages 98–99). Injuries need to be treated with orange at first, for a few days, to counteract shock. Then use indigo for tumors, blue for fevers, and red for malaise. Check the color acupressure chart for colors that treat specific ailments (see pages 109–113).

ENVIRONMENT: ORANGE

I have found that orange is generally a good color for all sick animals, from pets to livestock and wild creatures. Place the animal on orange bedding to provide comfort and security. Orange will also alleviate shock and fear. A warm orange glow from a light bulb can be used instead if the animal, such as a cow or a horse, cannot be placed on a blanket. It is wonderful to see a farmer up a ladder illuminating a huge barn with a sheet of orange cellophane covering the light to heal his animals. Tan, cream, and green can be introduced after the initial crisis has passed. Orange will also revive animals after the shock of delivery. If a newborn animal is abandoned or needs training, just shine a green light on its feet and gently tap its hooves or paws for 50 counts—it will of course bond to you!

Color Intake

Animals have the same need for basic color intake—through light or food—as humans. The color intake through their food is more limited in its color-range than humans, but just as necessary.

ORAL REHYDRATION: BRILLIANCE

Clear drinking water must be easily available to stop the animal dehydrating. The seven colors of the rainbow will be absorbed through the brilliance of water.

FOOD: BROWN AND GREEN

Keep food light and in small portions. Brown is the best color for the food as it keeps the animal grounded. Dark green can be introduced through herbs and grasses for the purpose of convalescence.

STRESS: BLUE

Pets can become stressed by simple challenges, such as the arrival of a guest or the noise of a vacuum cleaner, especially if they have not learned, since birth, how to interact with people and other animals. Prevent stress by introducing blue in a blanket or light bulb, for example.

AFTER HEALING: GREEN

Use your hands to infuse emerald green, or even wear green gloves. Then give the animal a healing pat—a pat from the heart.

DEMISE: PURPLE

When an animal has reached the end of its time, the inevitable has to be accepted. It's time for you to give the greatest show of love you can to your dear faithful friend. Let your love relieve physical suffering and stress. The blue and red comprising purple will quicken the transition in a state of peace and contentment.

Meditating with Color

MEDITATING WITH COLOR is a lovely, gentle way to prepare yourself for healing. Just a short time spent each day in meditation can bring about a deep relaxation which will open up your spiritual and physical bodies to receive the help you need. Everything starts to take on greater significance when you begin to experience the benefits of meditation. Your awareness is heightened to embrace life's energy forces in operation. You can meditate to turn up the purple flame of absolution and healing within you. Meditate to feed positive messages to yourself, which in turn are capable of restoring you to full health and a sense of well-being. Your vital force can be directed around your body to heal space centers. By visualizing color with your inner edge you can concentrate your thoughts.

A clear way of tapping into direction for our lives is through meditation, connecting to yourself and channeling cosmic energy. Energy follows attention; the attention you have given yourself by meditation creates "change." It gives you access to deeper realms of yourself, bringing you closer to your real self, and allowing you to become whole again. To receive answers using the aid of color while in a meditative state, ask the question and be aware of the color you think of after you have asked.

Meditation Preparation

You can meditate at any time and anywhere, but for best results choose the same time once or twice each day. Find a comfortable resting place, and lie or sit down, keeping the spine straight. Always keep the feet close to the floor to remain grounded and earthed. Try to meditate for 20 minutes, but even a few minutes is beneficial.

LEFT

Meditation with color is relaxing, and is a powerful preparation and focus for healing.

HEALING PURPLE FLAME MEDITATION

The purpose of this meditation is to use purple's energy to bring a wisdom and resurrection of the spirit for healing.

1. Relax body and mind starting with your toes and working up to your head. Focus on your breath. Keep a nice easy rhythm. Feel your body becoming heavier and heavier, but with your mind so light that it gently floats away.

2. Imagine pouring down from above a heavenly purple/violet light which fills the air around you. Concentrate your thoughts until you feel encapsulated by this shimmering beam.

3. Remain in this meditative state for at least 15 minutes of stillness, absorbing the purple haze of healing.

4. Suggest to yourself that you would like to be mentally and physically whole and healthy and repeat to yourself,

"every day and in every way I grow stronger and stronger." When you think positive statements, your heart and whole being respond to these loving instructions.

5. Finish the healing by allowing the purple mist to dissolve, and begin to focus on your breath. Begin taking deeper and deeper breaths until you become conscious of your body. Move your fingers and your toes, and, when you are ready, open your eyes. Rub your hands together very quickly until they become warm so that you are brought back to earth again. Sit quietly for a few minutes before moving. You will be given guidance eventually while meditating, if not immediately. Everything that you experience in the meantime is of value to you. You may find that during your meditation you feel uncomfortable; let whatever comes just be, and then let it go. We meditate to rediscover and heal ourselves. Regularly practiced, meditation can bring about a greater sense of peace and aliveness.

⑥ Beyond Color

Man is considered remarkable for his reasoning ability, yet humankind still hankers after methods that stimulate some mysterious faculty, enabling us to know things that are otherwise hidden. The art of divination is the method of predicting or indicating future events by methods of seeing beyond the usual senses. It can also be used for looking backward. It is an intuitive sense, with its own rationality and is available to all who trust in more than what is seen by the naked eye. When used in its purity, it can only benefit mankind, bringing comfort for those in need, and solace where there is unrest. It's all a matter of moving the self into a deeper consciousness of total awareness.

Divination and Color

COLOR IS PART of your divinatory physic make-up, as inherent as your sight or sense of smell. It is a sensitivity that we all have to a certain degree – the ability to fine tune the senses. The best way to find this sensitivity is to simply make yourself available and clear of mind, so that which was always there can be picked up. It helps to use color to connect you to the physic space. Tapping into your intuitive side means you have access to the whole.

Ancient mythology is full of the use of color with divination. Steeped in the awareness of the environment, the psyche, and the soul, the ancients knew that intuitive capacity is increased by the use of color – simply by harnessing its vibrations, seeing it, or thinking it. The Egyptian god Thoth used colors to stimulate and awaken the sensitive physic center in the head. You can do this by gently massaging the space between your eyebrows with the first two fingers of your left hand, while visualizing the color purple.

Soul Color

Because your soul is the foundation of everything that occurs in this life – and others – it is a good place to start. The soul is the very essence of life, the substance of a person. The breath can be linked to the soul in action, "the breath" being the shadow of the person. Some people see manifestations of spirits, believing that this essence is also soul energy. The color of the soul is considered to be blue while inhabiting the body. It reverts to clear brilliance upon demise. The soul color is constantly turning into other colors, or shades of gray or black when ill-health or wrong ways of thinking and conduct threaten its purity; in essence, when its bearer has lost the pathway of right living. Being in the blue – relating to the clear blue sky above – is literally preferred, it is man's trial throughout life to keep it this color.

LEFT
The indigo chakra space between the eyebrows can tap into the unseen "third" eye, the psychic center.

RIGHT
Divine your own personal soul-color through a simple meditative technique.

DISCOVERING YOUR PERSONAL SOUL COLOR

A very simple way to discover your soul color is to meditate on the breath, opening a channel of cosmic communication.

1. Sit or lie, and relax, focusing on your breath coming in and going out for 11 breaths.

2. Become aware of the space you enter before a breath is taken in or expelled – the U-turn before the beginning or ending of either of these actions.

3. Stay in this space for a while each time, and allow yourself to explore and go "walkabout."

4. After a few experiences, start looking for a color in your next U-turn space.

5. Remember this color, and when you're ready, open your eyes. Allow your personal celestial color to flash before your eyes for instant attunement. This color is the perfect color for you to tune in to, or to meditate with for a while before beginning any form of personal-growth work.

6. Read the appropriate section in Chapter 2, The Psychology of Color, to understand your soul's personal challenges.

Dowsing the Color Wheels

A GOOD WAY to access your intuitiveness is to use a pendulum with a color wheel. It's a wonderful way to have those important questions answered promptly. All you need is a piece of paper and a pendulum.

The Pendulum

A clear crystal pendulum is best, but a clear glass bead or button at the end of a piece of thread also does the job. To use the pendulum, hold the end of the thread between the first finger and thumb so that the crystal or button hangs down. Place the pendulum over the color wheel and ask it a question. If it swings in a circle to the right the answer is "yes," to the left it is a "no." If it swings backward and forward, it indicates that there is no conclusion, that the outcome could go either way. You can ask the question again later. Only ask one question at a time to avoid confusion.

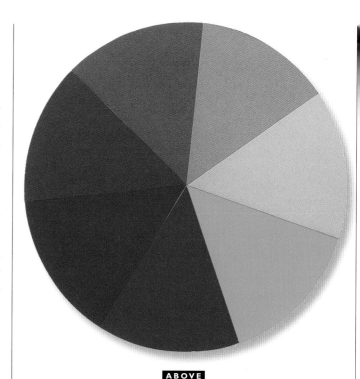

ABOVE
Use this color wheel for dowsing, or you can construct your own.

The Color Wheels

THE SPECTRUM-COLOR WHEEL

1. Use a clear pendulum when working with the general, spectrum-color wheel, which, as its name suggests, features all seven colors of the spectrum.

2. Take a large circle of white paper, divide the circle into seven pie-shaped sections. In each section put a spectrum color, one of the seven hues.

3. There are several ways of using the wheel. For general guidance, start by placing your pendulum in the center of the color wheel, and ask a question. Allow your pendulum to swing freely until it moves over to a color segment. Go to the color interpretation in Chapter 2, and allow your intuition to guide you while interpreting the color shown.

LEFT
Dowsing the color wheel can reveal new insights into problems, or give indications for the future.

THE SINGLE-COLOR WHEEL:

You may wish to focus on a specific area such as relationships or finance, both of which, as you will discover in the list on the right, relate to green. In this case you will need to make a single-color wheel. To give added weight to the single-color wheel, you can use pendulums with the same-colored crystals or buttons.

1. In Chapter 2, The Psychology of Color, check for the number of combinations, shades, and tints of green that are listed, including turquoise, which is blue-green. Construct a color wheel as previously, but using these variations on green.

2. Use the pendulum as before, to see which green it moves toward. Consult the color interpretations, as before. If it stops over pale green, then a new romance is possible. If dark green, your current relationship is stale. If emerald green, this is the right one! Turquoise implies that you are just a bit too much in love with yourself to share fully with another. If lime green, watch out for jealousy and envy.

3. You can construct a chart for any color area you wish. Use the list, right, for guidance on which color to use.

ABOVE

Crystal or glass pendulums of different colors are effective for dowsing.

LIFE-AREAS RELATING TO SPECIFIC COLORS

RED: travel, children, sex life

ORANGE: work, career opportunities, divorce

YELLOW: intellectual accomplishments, examinations, the media

GREEN: romance, money, finance, marriage, general health

BLUE: the healer, literary opportunities

INDIGO: house moves, psychic potential

PURPLE: leadership qualities, artistic possibilities, self-employment

Color Relate Reading

This color reading not only gives you information on earthly, mundane issues, necessary for everyday living, but also brings in your divinatory qualities. The beauty of the reading is that conscious ideas and opinions are not exchanged by sitter and reader. By choosing colors the sitter is working from a deeper level, more revealing than the spoken word. This gets to the core of the matter by exposing useless behavior patterns. It allows the inner mind to become flexible by using the "angle" of color. Using color results in images and analysis, giving as clear an association with the truth as possible. Color is a tool of self-discovery, and becomes the great corrective. When a color is selected, it is an indication of the internal needs that ultimately affect us on the outside.

We know that color enables us to communicate with the hidden parts of ourselves and others, and to uncover our own, sometimes hidden, agendas. If you can't understand why life doesn't work out for you, a satisfying career seems to elude you, or you don't get what you want out of a relationship, try the Color Relate Reading to help you through. The Color Relate Reading can cover every avenue and area you wish to pursue, whether it be from past lives, present-day issues, or insights into the future. The information can be found in Chapter 2, all you need now is the method, and to tune into your intuition to help you with your analysis.

You can give a reading by using a selection of colored cards that you can easily make at home. Make some of them with a single hue, and on others, draw a line across the center of the card, with the top half one color and the bottom half another. Be sure you cover all seven colors of the spectrum, as well as the shades, tints, and combinations listed in Chapter 2. The more colors used the wider the reading. When the two-color cards are placed for the reading, the top section represents conscious thoughts, and the action to be taken, while the lower half signifies subconscious thoughts, or what you would like to happen, but, as yet, has not taken place.

Color Relate Preparation

Assemble as many colors as you can. Put the cards in a group. Place the colors that will be chosen on a table before shuffling them. A pad and pencil is always a good idea so that notes can be recorded by the recipient.

Color Relate Method

It is crucial that the reader establishes in his or her mind the structure of the reading. In the Color Relate Reading, ten colors that the sitter likes are chosen, along with one color that is disliked. You may come across individuals who love every color, but there will be one that they are least drawn to. The client must not be hurried into making a choice—the colors can be handled and put back again. However, as each color is chosen, it cannot be changed once placed in position on the table.

FIRST THREE PLACES: SET UP

The first three groups of colors are the "set-up" places:

PLACE 1. KARMA: That which a person comes into this life with, the color you're born with. (See Karmic Color, page 128.)

PLACE 2. CHILDHOOD: Reveals the experiences that occurred in childhood.

PLACE 3. TODAY: Specifies where the person is within his or her life—right now, this minute, today.

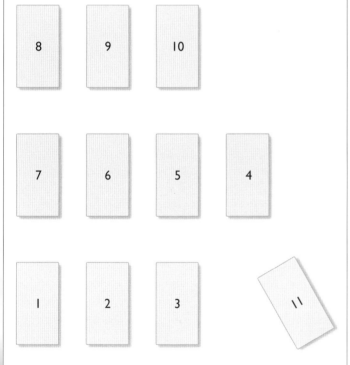

NEXT SEVEN PLACES: COMING IN, PLACES 4–10

The next seven color places indicate what could be coming in for the client over the next seven years—each place is a year. If you wish to go beyond the seven years just add more colors. In Chapter 2 you will find a number of interpretations for each color. Which aspect applies, and how that aspect applies, comes from the reader's intuition.

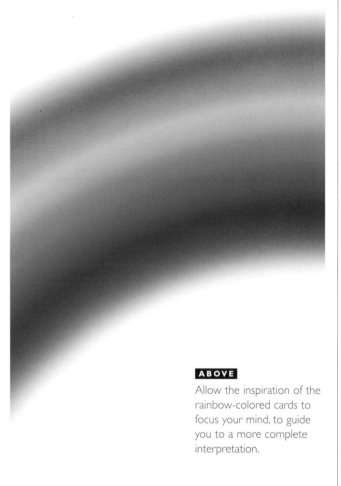

ABOVE

Allow the inspiration of the rainbow-colored cards to focus your mind, to guide you to a more complete interpretation.

DISLIKED COLOR PLACE: HINDRANCE, PLACE 11

The disliked color needs to be looked at while reading the next seven years for the client. This color shows what could hinder and cause disruption at some point—or for that matter, during this entire period. It is a very important placing, as taking note and acting on its information could turn around any adversity and disappointment, opening the way for positive growth. For example, if indigo is disliked, it could be saying that the sitter had better structure their life in more detail. Careless planning will not do—it is best not to leave things to chance.

LEFT

The Color Relate Reading covers everything in our lives from the past, present, and future.

Happiness and contentment flow from
self-knowledge and enlightenment.

Our past is written as surely in color
as in ancient words.

Karmic Color

The first color chosen in the Color Relate Reading is
the karmic color. In ancient Sanskrit, the reference to
karma is only one word: action. It is the only course in
life, everything moves and nothing stands still. The color
on the karmic place will give insight as to the essence
that the sitter came in with at birth, a guide to their path
in this life. For example, if a person's karmic color is blue
and they have an extremely busy, hectic life, then they are
running around for nothing—that is not what they are
meant to do! Blue is a color of contraction, not
expansion. The person may have abilities that can only be
developed by quietly working alone, such as writing.
Again, the intuition of the reader will uncover which of
the color aspects apply.

ABOVE
Recognize the hidden colors in your Relate reading for a complete understanding.

LEFT
The unchosen colors of orange and lilac in this reading also give valuable insights and information.

The Challenge of Hidden Colors

Some colors are combinations of other colors. If you find the information is not forthcoming with a chosen color, you can try reading it on the hidden level only. Take into account all unseen colors—they will give valuable insight. For example, when purple is chosen, do not ignore the hidden red and blue that is in it. With colors such as orange, green, purple, and turquoise, the color combinations must be taken into account if an obvious answer is not forthcoming.

Unchosen Colors

During a session, clients often omit one or more of the seven spectrum colors. The left-out colors show the deepest challenges over the seven-year period. For example, orange is the most rejected color. A dislike of orange shows a fear of moving forward, which an infusion of red will rectify.

Dislike of Color—Black Rainbow

It is very rare for an individual to say that they do not like color at all! But it can happen. A person who shuns color by positively avoiding it has a deep need for comfort. Somewhere in their lives they were pained emotionally to such an extent that they pushed away the light: the Black Rainbow, where everything appears desolate. Confidence and trust has been lost, and the person will need gentle persuasion to join the human race again.

Scrying

SCRYING IS DIVINATION by peering into any reflective surface. The word scrying means "seeing," seeking the future in a special way through transparent materials such as water, mirrors, or crystals, in which are formed visions, symbols, pictures of time coming in. Just about every culture has, at some point, employed various forms of scrying for divination—particularly when they were worried about the future. Working with the crystal ball's reflections, you are engaging the brilliant light where all colors come from. The brilliance gives a glimpse into infinity, wherein are contained all things.

Michel de Notre Dame (1503–1566), better known as Nostradamus, is perhaps the most famous seer of all time. His prophecies included the Great Fire of London in 1666, the French Revolution, Napoleon's defeat at Waterloo, Hitler's rise to power and his defeat, the atom bomb, plus many more. All of this by gazing for great lengths of time into a brass bowl of water resting on a brass tripod. For individual, future guidance or insights, he used a looking glass.

Colored Viewing

The popularity of crystal-ball gazing has always been its simplicity—much easier than the complex rituals that other means of divination sometimes employ. History reveals that elaborate rituals and preparations were often required, but the modern-day technique for scrying is much easier. A quartz crystal ball has always been a favorite tool for clairvoyant work.

Wealthy scryers of the past used a stone called beryl, of which emerald and aquamarine are variants. You can use these stones today if you are able to afford a piece the size of an orange! Beryl is usually green tinted, influencing the reading. The green will focus on new beginnings and happenings, such as business projects and new romances, rather than events likely to happen hundreds of years hence.

Dr. Dee, the court astrologer to Queen Elizabeth I of England, used a black Mexican obsidian the size of an egg. The queen would make no decision without first consulting her court scryer. In 1696, the famous seer John Aubrey suggested that the ball used for divination ought to have a tint of red, encouraging "pictures in the fire to be seen"—similar to staring into the embers of a glowing fire, thought to quicken happenings and speed up events. It was believed that the stronger the color used for scrying, the more the events were likely to be hastened. Black or colorless balls were thought to only have the ability to span backward and forward in time, without influencing events.

Tools

The equipment for basic scrying is a clear crystal ball made of glass or quartz. A stand will also be required to stop the ball from rolling around. Natural substances such as brass or wood are best. A glass or bowl of water, a

ABOVE
The mineral beryl was the material of choice for the well-to-do crystal gazers of the past.

ABOVE
Total concentration is required while delving into the realms of light.

mirror, or any reflective surface will substitute— or even staring into a pond or lake, as they are so fond of doing in fairy stories! You will need a table to put the object on, and a black cloth to cover the table, although a white cloth can be used.

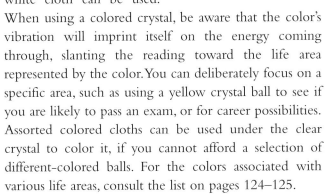

When using a colored crystal, be aware that the color's vibration will imprint itself on the energy coming through, slanting the reading toward the life area represented by the color. You can deliberately focus on a specific area, such as using a yellow crystal ball to see if you are likely to pass an exam, or for career possibilities. Assorted colored cloths can be used under the clear crystal to color it, if you cannot afford a selection of different-colored balls. For the colors associated with various life areas, consult the list on pages 124–125.

Never let anyone else touch your seeing equipment, and always wrap the crystal ball in black or purple velvet after use. Then put it in a dark-colored box and store it safely away in a drawer.

Location

You need a quiet room or other area that is not cluttered with junk. If the drapes are closed then two candles can be used for light—preferably white in brass holders. It is imperative that all utensils, and the room itself, are spotlessly clean. Dust hinders psychic phenomena. Two chairs will be needed, one for the seer and one for the sitter. It is best not to have more than one person for a sitting, but an exception can be made for someone to act as a support for the sitter if that would be more comfortable.

Time of Day

The best and traditional time is when the moon is waxing. The process works best when the sun is in the farthest northern position, but provided the body is relaxed and the nerves are calm to allow concentration, readings can be done at any time. Think of gold to steady the psyche and encourage a successful reading.

LEFT
Gazing into a bowl of water or other reflective surface is an alternative scrying technique.

ABOVE LEFT
The transparency of the crystal ball embodying the brilliance allows insightful reflections to be revealed.

Crystal-Clear Preparation

You are the only person who should handle your crystal ball. Cleanse it by gently washing it in a little white vinegar and tepid water and polish it dry with a velvet cloth or chamois leather. Never expose it to extreme temperatures, and do not expose it to direct sunlight. Moonlight is beneficial. A dimly lit room is required and it is best that the sitter is opposite you. You can hold the crystal in your hand or put it on a stand. Do not worry if you cannot see anything at first—it comes easily to only five people in every hundred. Practice and perseverance will help to develop any latent powers, enabling you to become sensitive and receptive.

Colored Misty Clouds

Scrying is a valid and active way of developing clairvoyance. All that enters its realm will be recorded

Reflective tools enable us to catch a glimpse into infinity.

and shown back to you. It is rare to see whole scenes or pictures—only the gifted psychic will do so—but a misty impression is often all that is needed to give you a lead into interpretation. You may be fortunate enough to get insight even with black, white, and gray clouding. Be patient, stay with it—it could become a color impression, giving further guidance on interpretation. Because other images or impressions will be self-explanatory, the minimum image of colored clouding is explained here. When staring into a crystal or the chosen reflector, it is usual to see a milky-white hue.

Black and White Clouds

Allow the mist to transform to reveal shapes, symbols, or even pictures. Black and white are usually the first colors to be seen. White clouds indicate peace and contentment. Black clouds may mean trouble ahead, a time to take extra care. You will eventually pass through this seemingly foggy stage to find meanings in the mist.

Ascending Clouds

Yes to any questions.

- **Red, orange, and yellow**—extreme activity—positive.
- **Green**—life is looking good—stable.
- **Blue, indigo, and purple**—aim to become self-employed.

Take the lead, you have the wisdom and experience.

Red, Orange, and Yellow Clouds

A lot of energy will be needed for endeavors to come to fruition. It would be wise to think before you leap into any situation. Should be on the move—not static. Good health.

Descending Clouds

No to any questions

- **Red, orange, and yellow**—nasty fall from life's position—careless and hasty. A closure to a project is nearer than you think.
- **Green**—money going out faster than coming in.
- **Blue, indigo, and purple**—delusions of grandeur, loss of opportunities, disappointment.

Blue, Indigo, and Violet Clouds

A time to reconsider and structure your life in a positive manner. It's possible to acquire all that is desired if careful planning is followed. Be careful not to get stuck in a rut.

Green Clouds

Money should be stable. Look to relationships and encourage love. Prosperity for the home, and progress in all endeavors.

Clouds Moving to the Left

Positive energy about to move away.

- **Red, orange, and yellow**—too late—missed opportunities—cancellations.
- **Green**—money running out—jealousy about you.
- **Blue, indigo, and purple**—not the time to push forward or ask for promotion.

Clouds Moving to the Right

- Good omen, support is at hand.
- **Red, orange, and yellow**—not long to wait for results.
- **Green**—good time to ask for a loan—comfortable.
- **Blue, indigo, and purple**—able to stand up and be recognized.

Dream Colors

DREAMS REVEAL THE deeper levels of personal existence. Where does the light come from to illuminate your dream? You are in a dark room with your eyes shut, sound asleep. Something is stimulating the light, it comes from somewhere! In the dark secret of the womb springs forth the eternal light. In the black there is light. The body of light was always with you, your dreams are the proof of that. In ancient Egypt dreams assumed a far greater significance and played a very important role in human affairs. Sleeping in a temple to obtain divine advice through a dream, or to obtain a cure by dream contact with a healing god, was known as an "incubation period." The dreams they experienced made men aware that they were constantly in contact with a mysterious supernatural world, from which they might learn about their own destiny in this world and the next.

Color Indicators for Dreams

To dream in color indicates what's coming in the future. When the dream occurs in black and white, it represents the past, and shows that it is time to move on. A nightmare is a sharp reminder that the structure of the person's life has been sorely disrupted, and is still festering. It is like septicemia of the memory, needing persistent support to clear. When the color is weak in a dream it suggests that something needs to be looked at right away.

Color Symbols

Apart from the significance that psychoanalysts attach to dreams, ancient lore interprets them symbolically, for the future of the dreamer or for those people he or she knows. To interpret your dreams, use the color aspect of the images from Chapter 2. Depending on their appearance and contents, dream images can be favorable or not. For example, a full plate of food indicates bountifulness, an empty plate the reverse. But always look for the color indication as well as its obvious symbolic significance.

There are many books of dream symbols, and you will be able to find within them interpretations for whatever appears in your dreams. None of them explore the color dimension, however. Because dreams are related to psychology, as is color, the colors which appear in your

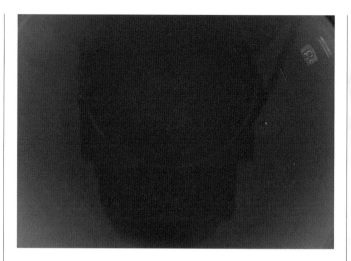

ABOVE
Dreams reveal themselves to your inner mind; be aware of the significant colors that manifest.

RIGHT
Let Cosmic Color Dreaming lead you into new facets of your own being.

dreams can be interpreted through the color psychology aspects discussed in Chapter 2. For example, obstacles such as doors that will not open suggest difficulties. Note the color of the door or its surrounding colors, and refer to Chapter 2 to give you clues as to what needs to be addressed to free up your life.

An example of a symbol that appears frequently in dreams is water, which, surprisingly, can appear in virtually any color. Note if the water in a dream is still, calm, or rough and what color it is. If it's turquoise and choppy it means affairs of the heart are in a period of turbulence; gentle movement suggests the personal relationship is moving along nicely; flat water shows a person is caged in their surroundings and unable to liberate themselves; rough gray water signifies that a person is trying to break those chains.

Cosmic Color Dreaming

You can open the color door to your own dreams through a simple process. Take a warm bath and afterward wear white attire and retire to white bed linen. On relaxing in bed, take easy breaths and visualize a huge diamond and its many-colored facets. Allow yourself to wander through the maze of clear, sparkling colors until you drift off into protected, safe, delightful dreaming, while absorbing the mystic light of creation.

Colored Candle Healing

A candle represents the light in the darkness. It also reminds us of the uncertainty of life, as it is easily extinguished. The candle's glow can lead the way even unto death—it is the divine light at the end of the tunnel, symbolizing the light without end, and our essential self. Candles cast light upon life's shadows, the flame illuminating the universe, and represent the vitalization of the sun. Fire has always been regarded as something holy, and it operates in all aspects of our lives, from the volcano to the fire of human passion and creativity.

Religions have used candles for centuries. Three candles joined together depict the holy trinity. The stem of the candle is suggested as the cosmic tree of life. In Kabbalism, Jewish mysticism, the three candles indicate wisdom, strength, and beauty. Candles have always been used as a part of ritual and initiation, and are primal connections to cultural solidarity.

Everything else takes on a greater significance when we start to experience the benefits of candle gazing. Once it has been experienced, our lives will never appear the same again. All thoughts and words spoken become clearer. You become aware of the operating of life's energies and learn the difference between what's important and what is not. The world can sparkle again and all can become possible. Colored candle meditation can set purpose in motion and is where prayers can be answered.

Using candles for healing is akin to creating a ritual fire—a process that has existed through the ages. The candle's glowing light warms and melts away negativity, enabling a restoration of health and well-being. A candle focuses the intention. An unlit candle represents the absence of life-giving energy, a lack of fire in the belly. Striking a match to ignite the flame sets fire to the soul, bringing in love and harmony.

Colored Candle Preparation

As a candle burns it releases and amplifies its own color energy. The colors start to infuse the immediate area and affect anyone who stands close by. Choose a candle in the color needed for the specific ailment or illness, or for happiness or good fortune. Check Chapter 2 or the color acupressure charts (see pages 109–113) for guidance.

Before using a candle, make sure it is clean. Cleaning the candle eliminates any unwanted vibrations that may have become attached during the time it was manufactured. It also ensures that the color of the candle can work to its full capacity. Simply wipe the candle with a tissue dampened with cool water and a little sea salt, starting from the wick end. You can anoint the candle with pure virgin olive oil, but use it sparingly. These preparations clear the way for the color to shine forth. You can reinforce the cleansing by repeating your intention several times, or by saying a prayer. Dressing the candle brings together the wax and the wick, symbolizing

the simple thread that runs through all our truths—color. It also unites you with the candle for the lighting rite.

Candle Timing

Any amount of burning time will be beneficial, but to get the most benefit, allow the candle to burn down to the bottom.

LEFT
The use of colored candles is a powerful way to infuse color healing energy.

ABOVE
Cleaning the candle before use ensures a fresh beginning.

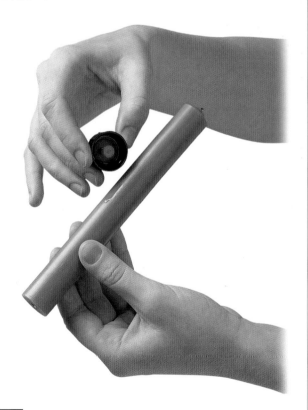

ABOVE
Anointing the candle with pure olive oil to allow the true color to shine.

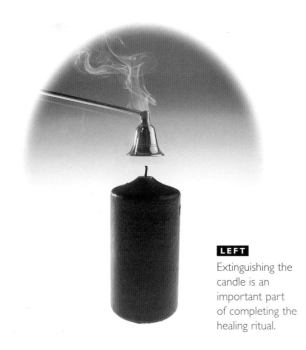

Candle Extinguishing

Never use your breath to blow out your candle as it is esoterically understood that one creative force should not be used to darken another. The extinguishing process should be regarded as a completion of the healing act, holding and securing the colored energy force. The candle can be put out by any small metal or china cup. It would be nice to acquire an old-fashioned candle snuffer, but even a home-made tin foil cone can be used.

Super Rainbow Candle Healing

Lighting a colored candle releases its energy into the atmosphere. The color vibration is absorbed into your auric field (see pages 96–97) and transmitted into your body. This multicolored process tops up the body with all the colors needed for a general health healing.

1. Place a candle of each of the seven colors of the rainbow in a semicircle before you, working from left to right—start with red on the left and finish with purple on the right. The candles can be placed either on the floor or on a table.

2. Sit quietly for a few moments in order to prepare yourself to receive.

3. Light all the rainbow candles in order, starting with the red. Beginning with the central green candle, gaze upon each flame for one minute at a time. Then move to the red candle on the left of the semicircle, and then to the purple on the right. Continue by going on to the orange and the indigo, followed by the yellow and finishing with the blue. This process should take seven minutes.

4. Let the candles remain burning and embrace all the colors as you will, allowing your higher self to guide you as to which of the colors to linger on. Continue for another ten minutes, finishing with the green candle that you started with, to balance your system.

5. Extinguish the candles in order, starting from the red.

6. Sit quietly for three minutes with your eyes closed, to complete healing.

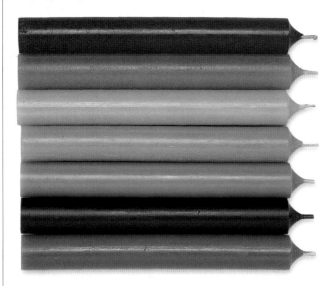

Single-Color Healing

The same rite can also be performed with candles of a single color. Select a color on the basis of the color properties described in Chapter 2.

Millennium Colors

As we enter the next thousand-year period, questions naturally arise regarding the future. So what does color have to tell us about all this?

First and foremost, color is an energy of nature and the natural world. The new millennium is purely an event of man, and far from being one for all men. However, an event that has recently taken place is related to the cycles of nature and the cosmos, and the place of the Earth itself within those cycles. That event is the entry into the Age of Aquarius. The color of the Aquarian Age is blue, representing the spirit of truth. We are all born in truth. As babies we know nothing else but the real self, being

Numerology for the Year 2000: Setting the Tone for the New Millennium

TWO—ORANGE

The number two relates to the color orange, which brings with it fantastic opportunities all-round. Of course, changes have to occur first. Orange is the great rejuvenator and ushers in extreme optimism. The orange of the number two encourages achievement. On the downside, orange can bring disruption and depression. It can also usher in the "reverse rainbow," which means we loose out on the experiences of life through trying to run before we can walk. Two is a primary and female number, and endows those who operate under it with a sweet nature, helpfulness, gentleness and modesty. But two also

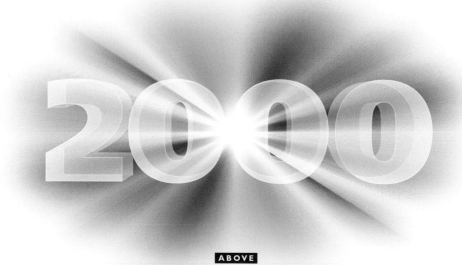

ABOVE
As the new millennium unfolds, the brilliant spectrum
continues to work its healing power.

perfect and positive. We acquire a false self because we have to adapt to survive. In this process we can loose our identity. The challenge of Aquarian blue is to strive constantly to discover and connect to the truth of ourselves.

This blue, scientific age is reviving lost wisdoms and healing arts from before. The color blue is the carer and healer, combating pain and cruelty. Blue's philosophical thinking will be working on a higher spiritual level, which blue will provide with the passing of years. Clearly there is a long way to go, but then, the Aquarian Age has seen us through the end of the last century and into this new millennium.

has a strong negativity, resulting in cruelty and deceit—it is fortuitous that the blue of Aquarius is with us to help restore balance to number two's negative orange traits.

ZERO—RAINBOW BRILLIANCE

The symbol of zero is disregarded numerologically, where it stands for emptiness and non-existence. However, the zero circle is one of the most powerful and widely used spiritual symbols. It is related to the brilliant light, containing all the colors necessary for developing full potential. A circle gives protection against evil. A zero is the perfect circular motion, the complete whole,

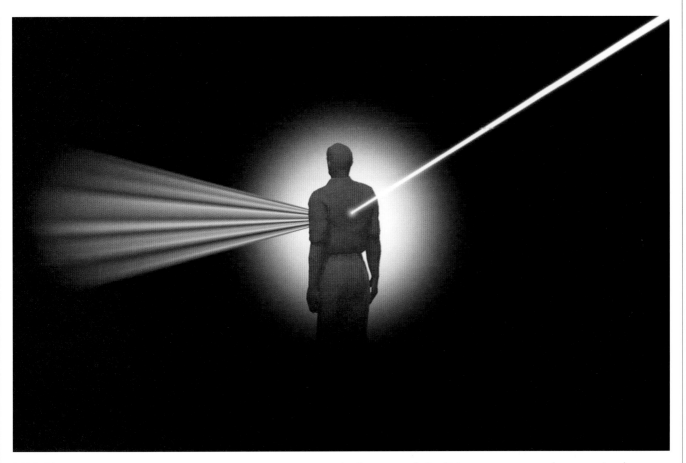

ABOVE

The brilliance coupled with blue and orange springboards us into the new millennium with peace and positive changes.

1. RED—fast—itchy—coverage—showy—stamina

2. BLUE—cold—light—quiet—kind—trustworthy

3. YELLOW—sharp—happy—crazy—lazy—lovely

COLOR TEST INTERPRETATION

No. 1 circle is how you see yourself
No. 2 circle is how others experience you
No. 3 circle shows who you really are, your true self

linking the universe together in unity. The zero brings about inner preservation which maintains your soul energy. You can make changes when you embrace spirit culture that gives direction.

Millennium Self-Color Test

To discover who you really are and how you relate to others and the world use the three zeros color test, taken from the year 2000. This process puts you through the hoop, the infinite space in the middle of the circle. Draw three zeros in a line underneath each other and fill in the first circle with a color, then write down five words that describe that color. Do the same for the next two circles. Don't read the interpretation until you have finished your colors and words. For example:

Use your mind and body as a prism to find your true colors for the 2000 millennium. Color will have an effect on future civilization; when used correctly it can reverse the tide. We are united by color. It takes on a form from its inner nature. For those who seek, color becomes a glorious influence, fulfilling promises for the future. Color vision is exquisite.

Know what color can do for you. It can change your life.

References

Birren, Faber, *Color Psychology and Color Therapy* (Citadel, 1961)

Nunn, John, *Ancient Egyptian Medicine* (British Museum Press, 1996)

Rendel, Peter, *The Chakras* (Aquarian, 1979)

Varley, Helen, ed., *Color* (Marshall Editions, 1983)

Verner-Bonds, Lilian, *Color Healing* (Random House, 1993

Useful Addresses

For further information on products and services mentioned in the text, contact the following addresses:

Lilian Verner-Bonds
The Colour-Bonds Association
137 Hendon Lane
Finchley
London N3 3PR
United Kingdom
Tel/fax: 020 8349 3299
for courses, private readings and training, postal readings, books, and *The Healing Rainbow* tape

The Oracle School of Colour
9 Wynsdale Avenue
Kingsbury
London NW9 9PT
United Kingdom
Tel/fax: 020 8204 7672
e-mail: pauline@oracleschool.fsnet.co.uk
for courses, color-crystal torches, and other color products

Olive Dewhurst Maddox
47 Kentford Road
Kents Bank
Cumbria LA11 7BB
United Kingdom
Tel: 01539 532875
for sound and color healing

The Color Association of the United States
589 Eighth Avenue
New York
New York 10018-3005
Tel: 212 372 8600

Author Profile
Lilian Verner-Bonds is an international author, lecturer, teacher, and healer. She has written books on color, color-zone therapy, and palmistry. Her tape, *The Healing Rainbow*, is regarded as a classic. Her work is widely recognized throughout Australia, Europe, and America. She is vice-president and past Chairman of the International Association of Color Therapists, and a member of the House of Commons Committee on Complementary Medicine.

index

Acknowledgments

Special thanks go to
Francis Annette, Carla Carrington, Dina Christy, Sally Craig, Frankie Goldstone, Anne Harrington-Lowe, Isabel Milne, Clive Oxley, Sharon Sephton, André Touhey, Sonja Wirwohl
for help with photography

With thanks to
Bright Ideas, Lewes
King's Framers, Lewes
Spellbound and Spirit, Lewes
Tie Rack, Brighton
Tizz's, Lewes
for the kind loan of props